THE CO

SOCCER

RESTART PLAYS

by
Mario Bonfanti
and
Angelo Pereni

Library of Congress Cataloging - in - Publication Data

Bonfanti, Mario and Pereni, Angelo
 The Complete Book of SOCCER RESTART PLAYS
  Original title: "CALCIO: Palla inattiva"

ISBN No. 1-890946-14-1
Library of Congress Catalog card Number 98-065649
Copyright © June 1998

First published 1996 by Editoriale Sport Italia Srl Milano Original title:
"CALCIO: Palla inattiva"

Reedswain Books are available at special discounts for bulk purchase. For details, contact Reedswain at 1-800-331-5191.

Editorial coordination
Marco Marchei

Translated from Italian by
Maura Modanesi

Art Direction, Design and Layout
Kimberly N. Bender

Editing and Proofing
Bryan R. Beaver

Printed by
DATA REPRODUCTIONS
Auburn Hills, Michigan

REEDSWAIN BOOKS and VIDEOS
612 Pughtown Road
Spring City, Pennsylvania 19475 USA
1-800-331-5191 • www.reedswain.com

This book is dedicated to our wives,
who, showing great sympathy
and spirit of self-sacrifice,
kindly allowed us
to cultivate a second 'passion':
playing soccer.

TABLE OF CONTENTS

FOREWORD

I am delighted to introduce this original book focused on a specific theme: restart plays from dead ball situations in soccer.

My long experience, as a soccer player and then as a professional coach, helped me to understand how important it is to coach these particular play situations, both in defense and in attack.

A team very often wins a match because it gives great care to tactical details during the training session, or it is often defeated because these details are not given the required attention. During the last few years, I had the luck to obtain important results with the youth team ("Primavera") of Atlanta soccer club: winning the Italian championship, Italian Cup and the international youth tournament in Viareggio (Tuscany).

In my opinion, we got these excellent results because my players were particularly close to each other - there was good understanding and great cooperation among them. They were also able to concentrate in the right moment, so as to combine their intents to achieve the same goal, both in the defensive and in the offensive phase.

In modern soccer, more than 50% of all the goals are scored at set plays or on directly consequent combinations.

Today, the actions following a corner, a throw-in, a direct or indirect free kick, are more and more dangerous. For this reason, every coach should suggest a series of suitable tactical schemes to help his players to memorize and manage the highest number of play variations deriving from dead-ball situations. Every coach should also offer his players the proper tools to tackle every tactical problem of the team in a competent and original way. This work written by Bonfanti and Pereni - two important authors already known in Italian and foreign soccer circles for their acknowledged competence - offers a wide range of set play exercises, which will undoubtedly raise the readers' curiosity to know more and their desire to create their own personal and original exercises.

Cesare Prandelli
Professional Soccer Coach in the Italian Serie 'A'

INTRODUCTION

The systematic study of soccer play in the last few years shows that restarting the game at set plays, whatever the situation, is often the main cause for goal scoring.

Whatever the competition level, the percentage of goal scoring is always very high in both cases: goals scored directly at free kicks or in directly consequent combinations. The high number of available stationary ball situations offers every team the possibility to condition the result of the performance positively - if the team is able to exploit these situations in the best way. This is possible only if the team in question has acquired effective skills in the execution and can control the play with particular and proper timing.

Every coach, as well as every team group, should follow their own methodology for coaching and learning free kicks.

With this book we intend to offer support and a contribution, which is the result of our long research and of the personal coaching experiences we acquired throughout the years. We are confident that our considerable work will act as an incentive for our readers, leading them to investigate the theme to find more and more suitable and original technical-tactical solutions.

The first chapter of the book deals with a very topical and modern subject: 'Comparing different team games', a theme which is leading many coaches and teachers involved in different sports to search for new material and stimulating confrontations.

The second chapter points out some historical periods which characterized the evolution of soccer play, with particular attention to the important moments that marked the birth and the improvement of the rules concerning the restarting of the game at set plays.

The third chapter is completely focused on a series of exercises explaining all the different ways to resume the game, laying emphasis on the relevant technical-tactical evolutions.

All the exercises are illustrated with written and graphic descriptions, where the static-dynamic positions of the players in question are given particular attention.

Finally, we did not forget to suggest some opportune lineups and the relevant defensive walls. We think it useful for our readers to end this work with a glossary and a bibliography for a possible further analysis of the theme.

Mario Bonfanti and Angelo Pereni

COMPARING DIFFERENT TEAM GAMES

For some years, sports scientists have been concentrating their attention on the importance of the 'transfer' in the performance of sports activities.

A long series of meetings, debates and, last but not least, all the books already published, allow us to realize the complexity of this problem from a cognitive point of view. This complexity implies constant updating and confrontations for every coach and educator, and, sooner or later, obliges them to raise serious questions for which they cannot always find satisfying answers. For this reason, it is necessary to go beyond every form of selfish, narcissistic and sterile knowledge. Today, qualified and highly motivated coaches feel it necessary to share their ideas concerning their own experiences on the field and their sports careers. Moreover, they understand the importance of alternating their research, combining theoretical knowledge with practical experience and creating and suggesting new exercises, so as to deduce general theoretical considerations.

The development of the studies in psychology applied to sports led to a more and more subtle differentiation between two important concepts: movement and action. Movement is a word defining a change in the position of a body in time and space, while the term action refers to all the mental activities - cognitive, motivational, emotional and relational - which, together with motor-sensorial processes, help a person to achieve set goals (Diagram 1).

Team sports, such as soccer, basketball, team handball and volleyball, require systematic training for play situations.

In general, the word situation is used to define all the components characterizing every sports activity (number of players, opponents, size of the field, space relations, athletic tension, etc.).

In addition to this definition it is possible to offer another explanation of the term from a subjective point of view; in this case, the expression 'play situation' refers to all the individual behavioral factors an athlete adopts in particular environmental circumstances, while trying to reply in the most rational way to the technical-tactical questions he is committed to on that specific occasion.

Recently, many theorists in sports sciences have been focusing their attention on a particular facet of the theme, analyzing how, why and to what extent it is profitable to transfer identical elements from one exercise to the other, from one performance to the other.

Definition of movement:
"Act made by a body changing its position in space, moving in a given time interval and at a given speed".

According to the laws of physics:

Force is $\qquad$ $F = M \times A$

Work is $\qquad$ $W = F \times S$

Power is $\qquad$ $P = W/T$

$P = F \times S \quad$ but: S/T is velocity (V) so:

$$P = F \times V \atop T$$

Definition of action:
"Conscious and well-aimed movement of the human body or of a part of it"

Components of a movement:
• perception of the outward reality
• mental imagination
• choice of the suitable gesture
• resolution
• performance of the gesture
• verification of the movement made

Diagram 1

In this case there is a specific reference to psychological theories, such as psycho-analysis, behaviorism, cognitivism, and connectionism in order to try to justify, at an acquisitive level, the simultaneous coaching/learning of different collective team plays.

The improvement of one's sports abilities at different games is undoubtedly an important goal; but this is not enough in view of the specific sports performance. In fact, the situations of a match - in soccer, for instance - change repeatedly so that the young athlete cannot previously know them.

Actually, during his performance, the player has to face some realities which cannot be defined or predicted beforehand: the ball - and therefore its material, its surface and its atmospheric pressure - as well as the morphological conditions of the pitch, weather conditions, the light source, and the visibility degree.

Other doubts concern the technical-tactical behavior of the

opponents, of the referee and of the audience.

From a methodological and didactic point of view, it would be possible to state that new play abilities can be trained considering the following coaching progression:

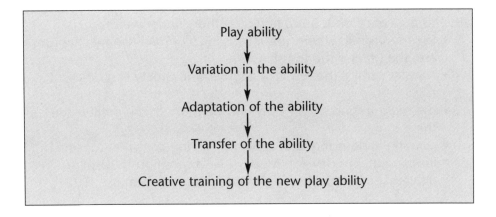

It is sometimes easy to confuse the concept of '**transfert**' with the concept of '**transfer**'. The former is a typically psycho-analytical concept, aimed at defining the kind of relationship which develops between the patient and his analyst. Anna Freud records some examples of transfert between children and animals, while other authors, belonging to psycho-therapeutic schools (M. Klein, H. Zulliger, R. Spitz, J. Bowbly, S. Isaac, E. Buxbaum, etc.), focus their attention on children's play. In their analysis they often discover traces of transfert on animals during children's activities or favorite games. On the contrary, the concept of transfer is connected to educational psychology. The word transfer means the effect of the performance of one current task on the following or previous one, like in the diagram below:

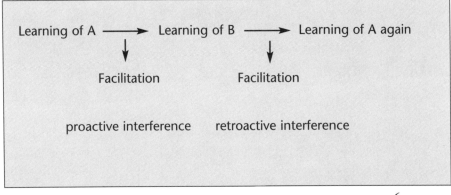

Classification of learning transfer

There is a question which is often recurring at different levels: is it possible to transfer in a team play the abilities acquired while performing other sports disciplines? Or rather: is it useful for a soccer player to play also basketball and volleyball? (See diagram 2).

All the answers are not affirmative, particularly as far as high-level athletes are concerned. But different authors underline that:

- the more similar their motor-sensorial coordinative mechanisms are, the greater the transfer.
- transfer can be the result of cognitive links between different tasks.
- the more frequently an activity is performed, the greater the transfer.
- learning various forms of activities sharing common aspects is fundamental to develop a particular disposition to acquire different sports abilities in variable situations (Famose, 1971).

Transfer
Ability to practice some exercises aimed at improving one particular skill, but which actually improve another one at the same time (Eberhart).

Examples:
- playing ball with one hand improves the ability of the other;
- observing somebody else play ball improves one's own ball playing;
- playing ball with one's hands indirectly improves ball playing with one's feet;
- practicing a sport improves one's sports and motor skills in other disciplines...

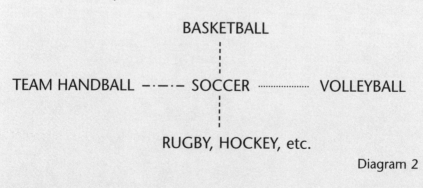

BASKETBALL

TEAM HANDBALL –·—·– SOCCER ················ VOLLEYBALL

RUGBY, HOCKEY, etc.

Diagram 2

However, it is proven that the more one is at the first stages of his/her motor learning, the more the transfer is effective.

Playing with one's right hand makes it easier to play with one's left hand and vice versa; in the same way, playing with one's hands helps ball playing with one's lower limbs and one's head.

The transfer while learning sports skills sharing the same motor features is possible and desirable, but it cannot replace highly-specialized particular training.

In short, it is possible to assert that performing different sports team games during childhood:

- makes it easier to improve one's anticipation ability;
- improves one's ideo-motor-sensorial reply;
- accustoms to mutual support;
- encourages cooperation;
- fosters the use and the understanding of non-verbal communication;
- stimulates one's inclination to learn;
- makes back-transfert effective, i.e. even adults are educated!

COMPARING THE FOUR TEAM GAMES
a. The ball and the playing field/court

Discipline	Circumference (in)	Weight (oz)	Playing field/Court (yd)
Basketball	30 - 31	20 - 22	28 x 15
Volleyball	26 - 27	8 - 10	19 x 10
Soccer	27 - 28	13 - 16	130 x 100
Team Handball	23 - 24	14 - 17	43 x 22

b. Body Contact

Discipline	Body contact	Progression
Basketball	light	gradual, while playing ball with one's hands
Volleyball	absent	without progression with the ball
Soccer	strong	free progression, ball playing with one's lower limbs and one's head
Team Handball	sharp	gradual, while playing ball with one's hands

c. Influence of the different energetic processes in the most important team games

Sports discipline	Aerobic process	Anaerobic process without lacitc acid	Anaerobic process with lacitc acid
Volleyball	Scarce	Maximum	Scarce
Basketball	Scarce	Maximum	Scarce
Team Handball (keeper)	Insignificant	Maximum	Insignificant
Team Handball (other roles)	Scarce	Maximum	Scarce
Soccer (keeper)	Insignificant	Maximum	Insignificant
Soccer (other roles)	Moderate	Maximum	Moderate
Rugby	Moderate	Maximum	Moderate
Field hockey	Moderate	Maximum	Moderate
Ice hockey	Moderate	Maximum	Moderate
Roller-hockey	Scarce	Maximum	Moderate
Baseball	Insignificant	Maximum	Scarce
Softball	Insignificant	Maximum	Scarce

d. Classification of the sports disciplines according to the duration of the competitions and to the required bio-energetic fea-

Sports Discipline	General Resistance	Aerobic Power	Lactic Acid Capacity	Lactic Acid Power	Alactic Acid Capacity	Alactic Acid Power
Volleyball	•		•	•	••	••
Basketball	•		•	••	•••	•••
Handball (keepers)	•			•	•	•••
Handball (other roles)	•			•	•••	•••
Soccer (keepers)						•••
Soccer (other roles)	••	•	•••	••	•••	•••
Rugby	••	•	•••	••	•••	•••
Field hockey	•		••	•	•••	•••
Ice hockey	•		•••	••	•••	•••
Roller-hockey	•		•••	••	•••	•••
Baseball	•		•		••	•••
Softball	•				•	•••

Three symbols (•••) mean the maximum importance given to the energetic process it refers to and, as a consequence, to the methods needed to develop the skill and/or the power in question.

Two symbols (••) refer to a moderate importance;

one symbol (•) stands for scarce importance.

Finally, the lack of any symbol represents the very little importance of the process while performing the discipline in question (Bellotti, Benzi, Dal Monte, Donati, Matteucci, Vittori,1993).

e. The kind of movement made by the ball in different sports games.

Discipline	Grazing	Bouncing	Air
Basketball	•	•	•
Volleyball			•
Soccer	•	•	•
Team Handball		•	•
Rugby	•	•	•
Hockey	•		

f. Restarting the game at set plays.

Basketball	Volleyball	Soccer	Team Handball
Center jump	Serve	Kick-off	Serve
Throw from end	Serve	Goal kick	Throw from endline line
Free throws	Serve	Penalty kick	7-meter throw
Jump ball	Serve	Free kick	Free throw
Jump ball	Serve	Corner kick	Corner throw
Throw from side	Serve	Throw-in	Serve at handout lines

g. Common tactical goals

Attack	Defense
• Retaining possession of the ball	• Regaining possession of the ball
• Gaining forward space	• Preventing the opponents from moving forward
• Achieving one's athletic goal	• Preventing the opponents from shooting at goal

THE DIFFERENT SPORTS DISCIPLINES. . . AT SOCCER'S DISPOSAL

A careful and repeated confrontation with coaches of other sports team-disciplines allowed us to draw the following series of specific movements, which can be transferred to soccer:

Track and field • circular-style running (leaning, push, stride...);
Soccer • circular running, avoiding flat running (heel pain, back-ache...).

Track and field • high jump (the last three steps);
Soccer • run and take-off with one foot, while playing ball with one's head or while saving high shots (goalkeeper).

Volleyball • space-time coordination;
Soccer • timely actions (timing).

Volleyball • acrobatic skills (dive, roll, save);
Soccer • low and high save; air play with one's feet or one's head.

Volleyball • dealing with space in area 1 and 2, in the middle, on the left and on the right
Soccer • ability to move in every area of the field: defense, midfield, attack (left and right).

Volleyball • receiving, tossing and attacking the ball - tactical antici-pation ability, the action goes on according to the success or the fail-ure of the attack: covering action;
Soccer • defensive tackle, pass, attack - tactical anticipation ability: ensuring the defensive balance while preparing the offensive action (numerical advantage over the opposition).

Basketball • give-and-go, give-and-follow;
Soccer • wall-pass, pass on an overlap run (inside and outside).

Basketball • L-play in defense;
Soccer • L-play in zonal defense.

Basketball • floating and forcing the driver away;
Soccer • committing the forward to one's teammate (floating) and forcing the opponent with the ball to move outside

Basketball • faking and screen while attacking
Soccer • feint and screen when restarting the game at set plays (corner kick, throw-in, free kick).

Basketball • rapidly gaining space forward, while shifting from defensive to offensive play (10-second rule);
Soccer • offensive action and shot at goal within a given time.

Basketball • double teaming on both sides in order to prevent any cross;
Soccer • defensive diagonal movement and double teaming.

Team Handball • common features while restarting the game at set plays: free throw, throw-in, penalty-throw; the goalkeeper's actions; common coordination and conditioning abilities: promptitude, speed, effective height, change of pace, change of direction, specific endurance; common tactical features: gaining space forward and sideways, also through backward passes (See Rugby), rapidly deciding on the best solution, according to one's teammates and to one's opposition.

Team Handball • 2 v 2, 3 v 3, 4 v 4, 5 v 5 play situations;
Soccer • 2 v 2, 3 v 3, 4 v 4, 5 v 5 play situations.

Rugby • touch and penetration;
Soccer • gaining space forwards through a backward pass.

Field hockey • play continuity and pressing all over the field;
Soccer • avoiding stagnant play; pressing all over the field.

RESTARTING THE GAME AT SET PLAYS

Historical background

The socio-cultural framework characterizing modern times leads people to feel unique protagonists of their historical age, as if the experiences of previous generations were not particularly important and significant: history is born with 'my personal history', the rest is of no importance!

This way of thinking is typical of young generations; however, in our opinion, it reveals two considerable ethical problems:

I am not interested in what the others do; only what I do is important!

Since there is nothing important before me, whatever I do or invent is original!

While reasoning in this way, we easily forget that many people before us, and probably more qualified than us, helped to improve this wonderful game of soccer, practiced and appreciated all over the world.

This chapter is dedicated to curious and attentive readers, motivated to improve their historical knowledge and aware that new and original ideas are the result of constant study, knowledge and control.

There is still a question under discussion: do the laws of the game condition tactics and skills, or vice versa? In other interesting works you can find a comprehensive and updated history of soccer rules; this chapter deals with some historical information concerning only the evolution of those rules regulating one specific aspect: Restarting the game at set plays.

The first official document including the laws of the game was drawn up by the English Football Association on 8th December 1863; it was made up of 14 articles.

Kick-off. According to this law: the game shall be started with a place kick from the center of the field, taken by a player of the team losing the draw. Every player of the opposing team shall remain not less than 10 yards from the ball until it is kicked off.

Only since 1902 has it been compulsory to mark out the halfway line across the field and a circle with a 10 yards radius around the center spot.

From then on, the kick-off rule underwent no practical changes, but some minor readjustments and interpretative specifications.

Goal kick. For the first time in 1877 there was a specific reference to the referee restarting the game after any temporary suspension of play from any cause not mentioned elsewhere in the Laws. Provided that immediately before the suspension the ball had not passed over the touch or goal-lines, the referee had to resume the game, 'throwing the ball upwards'. Only in 1908 was it decided that the ball should be 'thrown to the ground'; according to the laws now in force, the referee shall 'drop the ball' (Law #8). When the ball is played over the goal-line by a player of the team of that goal, a player on the same team has the right to take a free kick from the goal-line, at the point perpendicularly nearest to where the ball was first touched. The nearest opponent shall remain not less than 6 yards from the ball. This was the goal kick rule according to the Laws of the game drawn up in 1863.

In 1873, this law was radically modified: the team defending the goal had the right to resume the game only if the ball was last touched by an opponent before it crossed over the goal-line.

As years went by, the law underwent further changes: since 1913, the opponents must stand at a distance of 10 yards, until the other team takes the goal kick; since 1936, the ball is in play if it is kicked so as to move outside the penalty box towards the middle of the field; finally, since 1980, all the opponents must stand outside the penalty area until the ball is kicked outside the box - only then is the ball considered in play (Law #16).

Corner kick. There is something more to say about the theme concerning the above-mentioned goal kick rule. Actually, it is necessary to underline that if the ball was last touched by a defending player before crossing over the goal-line, the team attacking that goal was entitled to take a free kick from the nearest corner flag (Laws of the game drawn up in 1873). In 1880, it was decided to mark out the corner area, drawing a quarter circle having a radius of 1 yard from the corner of the field (the same size as today), and it was stated that there is no offside position at corner kicks.

In 1971, the International Football Association Board (IFAB) - the international body assigned to update and revise the Laws of the Game - underlined that the expression 'the whole of the ball shall be placed within the quarter circle' means that 'the projection of the circumference of the ball cannot get over the outward border of the boundaries of the corner area' (Law #17).

As long as there were no referees and linesmen controlling the match, free kicks did not exist. In case of a breach of the regulations, which were previously agreed upon by the captains of the two teams, the guilty player had to give the ball to his opponent, so as to resume the game.

Free kick or indirect free kick. In 1873, the International Board settled upon the cases in which the infringement of the Laws had to be punished by awarding a free kick. The expression 'free kick' refers to a place kick from which a goal cannot be scored unless the ball has been played or touched by a player other than the kicker before passing through the goal; today, it corresponds to an indirect free kick.

Direct free kick. The expression 'direct free kick' appeared in 1903; in this case a goal can be scored direct against the offending side. At the beginning, the distance between the defensive wall and the ball was 6 yards, but in 1913 it was increased to 10 yards.

This is a very complex law to enforce and often caused problems to referees; for this reason, it gradually underwent adjustments and revisions (Law #13).

Penalty kick. The penalty kick rule was introduced by the IFAB in 1891, on the suggestion of the Irish Football Association.

There were always many players crowding the areas near the two goals and, in order to prevent opponents from scoring, defenders often had to resort to using their hands, which was merely punished by awarding a free kick. Later on, before the penalty was taken, the referee had to listen to the reasons of the captain of the guilty team and, in case his arguments were considered well grounded, the referee could modify his decision.

Since 1902, the goalkeeper must stand inside his own goal-area; since 1929, the goalkeeper must stand on his own goal-line.

Since 1938, he must stand on his own goal-line, between the goalposts, without moving his feet until the ball is kicked.

Starting from 1986, the player kicking the penalty must be previously identified by the referee (Law #14).

Throw-in. In the course of the decades, the throw-in rule underwent considerable changes. Until 1863, players followed the ball beyond the touch-lines. The one who touched it first had the right to take the throw-in by kicking the ball directly on the field from the point where it previously crossed the line.

In 1863, it was decided that, after winning the ball outside the field of play, the player had to throw it using one or both hands; the throw had to be taken 'perpendicularly' to the touch-line.

In 1877, the 'right angle throw' was replaced by a throw taken in any direction of the field.

In 1880, it was added that no player is in an offside position at throw-ins. In 1887, the throw-in was awarded to the team opposite to that of the player who last touched the ball before it crossed the line.

Since 1898, a goal shall not be scored directly from a throw-in.

Starting from 1937, the thrower, at the moment of delivering the ball, must face the field of play and his feet cannot cross the touch-line completely (Law #15).

After this rapid overview of the history of the Laws of the Game, the previously unanswered question recurs again: do the laws of the game condition tactics and skills, or vice versa?

We are now absolutely persuaded that the debates producing changes in the laws are the result of all the experiences lived on the field. But once they have been introduced, it is just these rules which should foster the search for new and more suitable technical-tactical solutions.

Percentage of goals scored at set plays during USA 1994 World Cup

Team	Goals Scored	Goals scored at set plays	Percentage
Bulgaria	11	8	72
Italy	8	5	62.5
Brazil	12	5	41.5
Sweden	16	6	37.5
Germany	9	5	55
Romania	10	4	40
Argentina	8	4	50
Switzerland	5	3	60
Arabia	5	2	40

DIDACTIC MODEL AND JOINT LEARNING

Soccer coaches are used to saying that the quality of play often depends on whether technical-tactical details are given particular attention or not. It is common knowledge that 50% of all the shots at goal during a match are taken while restarting the game at set plays.

Tactical and strategic arrangements are often restricted to active play, while very little attention, particularly in youth sectors, is turned to training tactical schemes, performed when restarting the game at set plays: both in the defensive and in the offensive phase.

This book is aimed at helping coaches understand and work out play schemes relating to this theme. Obviously, we are perfectly aware that this is not an exhaustive report, but it can however help coaches improve their technical-tactical solutions and suggestions; it can be a support, above all, for coaches who are necessarily motivated to learn and bring themselves up to date.

In this context, we want to take into consideration some particular situations, characterizing the restarting of the game at set plays; these situations include:

Kick-off
Goal kick
Penalty kick   in offensive and
Corner kick   defensive play
Free kick
Throw-in

The team restarting the game in a set-play situation should consider some important behavioral aspects that we now break down as follows:

1 • **Importance of the player who restarts the game:** precision, anticipation ability, rapidity in finding alternative solutions, rapid communication.

2 • **Importance of those who perform the screen:** do not perform a passive screen, but an active one; self-sacrifice; timing of movements; ability to absorb 'dirty tricks'; do not infringe the rules; ability to conceal one's intents.

3 • **Importance of those who exploit the screen:** ability to perform diverting movements and to surprise one's opponent; determination while shooting at goal.

4 • **Importance of all the movements:** perfect synchronism of all the movements; precision while passing; ability to deal with different tactical alternatives; ability to anticipate one's opponent's movements; firm belief in one's tactical choice; ability to support the kicker, also after his shooting at goal.

The main technical-tactical components to achieve positive results are:

1 • Play organization.
2 • Surprise and possible alternatives.
3 • Exploiting the skills of one's players.
4 • Exploiting the weaknesses of one's opponents.
5 • Lapses in concentration during the first and the last minutes of the match.
6 • Firm belief in scoring the goal.

In order to be able to better learn and convey the tactical skills concerning play situations at set plays, this book offers a conventional didactic model which, in our opinion, is very useful if understood and used (Diagrams 3 and 4).

Diagram 3 shows a field of play on which tactical movements are outlined schematically; particular emphasis is given to the team retaining possession of the ball, which should be able to shoot at goal.

Our diagrams take into consideration the whole of the field and all the players, so that the coach can get accustomed to and gradually acquire a tactical view of the whole of the pitch. In order to help the reader to examine every single didactic diagram, we thought it useful to emphasize the area of the field where the most suitable shot at goal is likely to be taken.

Restarting the game at set plays:
.....................#

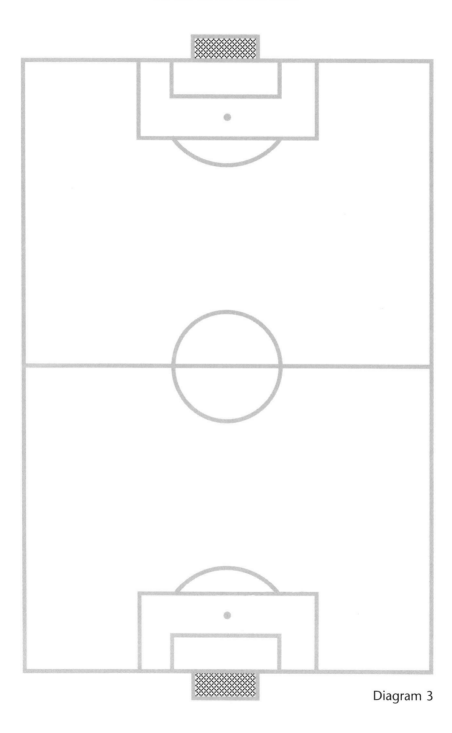

Diagram 3

Technical-tactical purposes:

_____

_____

Equipment:

Area required:

Coaching methods:

Description of the offensive situations:

_____

_____

_____

Common mistakes made by inexperienced players:

_____

_____

_____

Coaches notes:

_____

_____

_____

Graphic

- - - - - - ►	PATH OF THE PLAYER WITHOUT THE BALL
————►	PATH OF THE BALL
∿∿∿►	DRIBBLE
1, **2**, **3**,........	ATTACKING PLAYER
❶, **❷**, **❸**,........	DEFENDING PLAYER
□ ○ ————►	ATTACKING PLAYER WITH THE BALL
●]	FEINT
●[	SCREEN

Diagram 4

Diagram 4 is connected to the previous one and points out some useful aspects, which are the basic components of didactic planning (category, date, technical-tactical purposes, equipment, spaces available, coaching methods, description of the exercises and of the mistakes commonly made by inexperienced players), as it is possible to realize, while examining the examples offered in the following pages.

On other occasions, we have already had the opportunity to speak about the division of the coaching methodology into deductive and inductive methods.

The deductive method focuses the attention on the coach, who is the main protagonist of the training session. He explains all the different exercises; his players perform what they are told in a servile way and with unquestioning obedience. This method is further divided into three sub-groups, which are defined as follows:
- method of assigning tasks,
- mixed method (global-analytical-global),
- prescriptive method.

The inductive method underlines the importance of actively involving the player in the solution of technical-tactical problems, so that he becomes the protagonist in the development of the play. In this way, the coach explains the problems concerning a particular situation, leaving to his players the task of finding a solution (*). Also this:
- method is divided into three sub-groups:
- method of free exploration,
- method of guided discovery,

However, in no case can the coach forget his duties as an educator and teacher; actually, he can be involved by his players at any time, because the situation is getting complicated and they cannot find the possible dialectic solution (theoretical and practical) to the problem they had to cope with. Moreover, in this chapter we want to emphasize the importance of coaching soccer in a way as to involve the whole of the team group actively.

(*) We owe to Aristotle the analysis and the classification of the different forms of deduction; he identified deduction with syllogism, a didactic process proceeding from the universal to the particular, contrary to induction, starting from the particular to get to the universal. In this century, an American philosopher, Charles Peirce (1839-1914), revived the concept of deduction; he distinguished between analytical interference or deduction and synthetic interference or induction (Author's note).

It often happens that, during the training session, there is a conflictual psychological atmosphere between players of the same team; this negative situation cannot help learning, neither individual nor collective.

From the United States we are getting reassuring news about the didactic use of joint learning. It can be defined as a methodology of group learning, organized in such a way as to occur and be optimized thanks to a joint exchange of information and experiences between members of the same group.

Every single player is responsible not only for his own learning, but also towards his teammates who, like him, are concentrating on the performance and on the solution of specific tasks the coach assigned to the team. An important element characterizing this approach is the atmosphere of real cooperation within the team group in that particular environment.

Moreover, it is proven that joint learning has profitable effects on the development of positive social behaviors; on the cognitive progress, both of individuals and of the group; on the improvement in one's self-esteem and in interpersonal relations.

The main basic principles for joint learning are:
- positive interdependence,
- individual and joint liability,
- active and fruitful interaction between players,
- teaching of social skills, useful to interact within the team,
- elaboration and practical performance of the work carried out (Johnson, 1986).

By means of an active cooperation of the group, it is important not to repress the disagreements and contrasts which could break out during the learning phase. Actually, 'opposition and coordination, proper insight and encouragement, explanation and correction, social-cognitive conflict and mutual help, belong to the general category of the social elements fostering the acquisition of knowledge' (Pontecorvo, 1987).

It is convenient for a coach to reflect on these theoretical considerations every time he wants to suggest to his players any kind of exercise requiring joint work and cooperation between all the members of the team; one of these moments, very important from a tactical point of view, concerns coaching the restarting of the game at set plays.

SUGGESTIONS FOR PRACTICE

Exercises

In this chapter we will show you different exercises in various set play situations. The first part is mainly dedicated to preparing the offensive phase, while the second one concerns the setting of the defensive walls.

The diagrams shown in this book should not be considered as 'rigid information'; on the contrary, we hope that they will further stimulate the readers to create new and more original technical-tactical solutions.

Exercises	Number
Offensive phases	
Kick-off	6
Goal kick	9
Corner kick	22
Free kick	15
Penalty kick	5
Throw-in	13
Defensive walls	
Wall 4 + 1 at direct shot	1
Wall 4 + 1 at indirect shot	1
Wall 3 + 2 at direct shot	1
Wall 3 + 2 at indirect shot	1
Wall 2 +2	1
'Zone' arrangement at corner kick	1
Total	76

OFFENSIVE PHASES
Restarting the game at set plays:
Kick-off #1

Technical-tactical purposes:
Surprising the opposition by means of a diagonal rightward counter-pass.

Equipment: 6 balls; 11 + 11 colored shirts.

Area required: Regulation soccer field.

Coaching method: Deductive ➡ assigning tasks.

Description of the offensive situations:
- 9 takes the kick-off towards 10 .
- immediately ⑨ attacks 10 forcing him to make a back-pass towards 5 ;
- this player rapidly passes the ball to his teammate 11 , who makes a fast pass on the run of his teammate 3 , who is coming from behind
- 3 makes a direct counter-pass for the penetration of 7 , who controls the ball and dribbles for some yards; then he crosses the ball towards the far corner of the goal-area, where 11 is arriving
- 11 immediately shoots at goal, if possible with a diagonal shot aimed at the far post of the opponents' goal.

Common mistakes:
Lack in individual skills: ball control, pass...
Difficulty in performing suitable tactical synchronisms.

Coaching notes: ————————————————————————

———————————————————————————————————————

———————————————————————————————————————

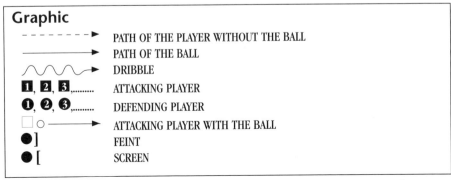

Graphic
- - - - - - - ▸ PATH OF THE PLAYER WITHOUT THE BALL
———————▸ PATH OF THE BALL
〜〜〜〜▸ DRIBBLE
1, **2**, **3**,......... ATTACKING PLAYER
❶, **❷**, **❸**,......... DEFENDING PLAYER
☐ ○ ———▸ ATTACKING PLAYER WITH THE BALL
●] FEINT
●[SCREEN

Restarting the game at set plays:
Kick-off #2

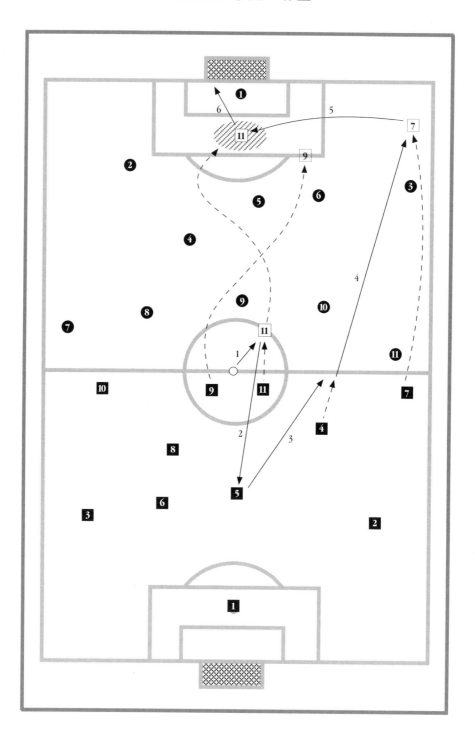

Technical-tactical purposes:
Conquering space forward and sideways.

Equipment: 6 balls; 11 + 11 shirts of two different colors.

Area required: Regulation soccer field.

Coaching methods: Inductive ➻ free exploration.

Description of the offensive situations:
- the player 9 starts the game with a diagonal pass to 11 ;
- 11 plays the ball to 5 , who immediately passes to 4 ;
- 7 sprints on the right wing to receive an end-to-end pass from 4 ;
- 7 gets possession of the ball and makes a fast cross towards the penalty spot for the running 11 ;
- 11 , or 9 if the pass is short, runs to meet the ball and shoots at goal towards the near post

Common mistakes:
The pass to 7 is not taken in the direction of his run.
The cross-over play of 11 and 9 in the offensive action is too slow.

Coaching notes:_____

_____

_____

_____

_____

_____

_____

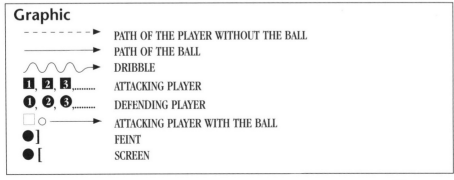

Graphic

- - - - - - - ➤	PATH OF THE PLAYER WITHOUT THE BALL
⎯⎯⎯⎯➤	PATH OF THE BALL
∿∿∿➤	DRIBBLE
1, **2**, **3**,........	ATTACKING PLAYER
❶, **❷**, **❸**,........	DEFENDING PLAYER
☐ ○ ⎯⎯➤	ATTACKING PLAYER WITH THE BALL
●]	FEINT
●[	SCREEN

Restarting the game at set plays:
Kick-off #3

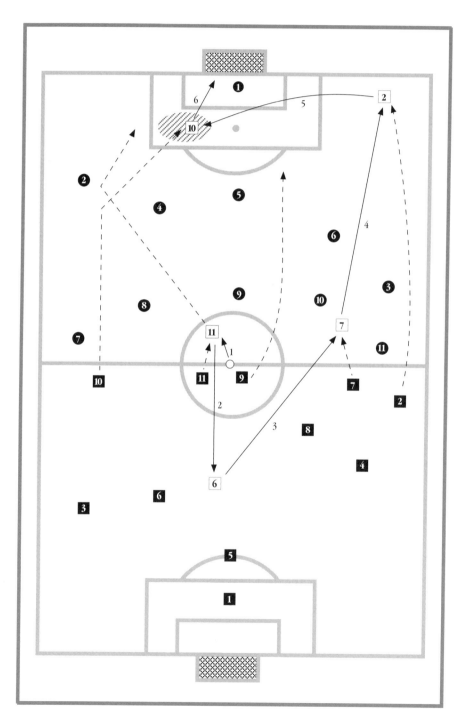

Technical-tactical purposes:
Kick-off with back pass.

Equipment: 3 + 3 balls; 11 + 11 colored shirts.

Area required: Regulation soccer field.

Coaching methods: Inductive ➤➤ guided discovery.

Description of the offensive situations:
- the forward ⑨ kicks off, passing the ball forward to ⑪;
- who makes a back pass to ⑥.
- ⑥ makes a diagonal pass into the run of ⑦;
- ⑦ controls the ball and makes a penetrating pass for ②, who is sprinting from behind on an overlapping run
- from the goal-line, ② crosses the ball with his right instep for the unexpected penetration of ⑩, who previously performed a cross-over play with ⑪.

Common mistakes:
Difficulties in receiving and controlling the ball while moving

Coaching notes:
_____

_____

_____

_____

_____

_____

_____

_____

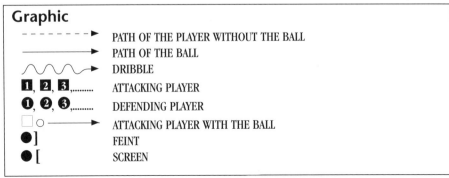

Graphic

‒ ‒ ‒ ‒ ‒ ►	PATH OF THE PLAYER WITHOUT THE BALL
——————►	PATH OF THE BALL
∿∿∿►	DRIBBLE
1, **2**, **3**,.........	ATTACKING PLAYER
❶, ❷, ❸,.........	DEFENDING PLAYER
☐ ○ ——►	ATTACKING PLAYER WITH THE BALL
●]	FEINT
● [	SCREEN

Restarting the game at set plays:
Kick-off #4

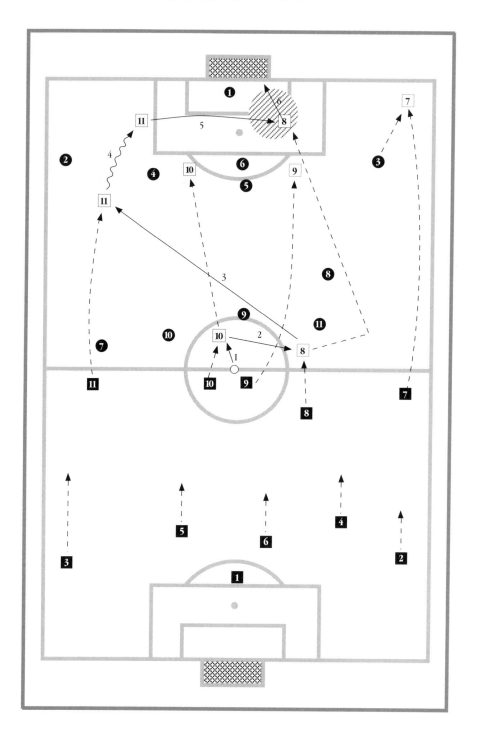

Technical-tactical purposes:
Different players performing overlapping runs.

Equipment: 3 + 3 balls for the 2 goalkeepers; 11 + 11 shirts.

Area required: Regulation soccer field.

Coaching methods: Deductive ➤➤ mixed.

Description if the offensive situations:
- 9 kicks off leftward to 10 ;
- 10 immediately passes the ball to the running 8 , who makes a first-time pass for the penetration of 11 on the left wing
- 11 dribbles the ball for some yards and then makes a flat cross towards the edge of the goal area for the running 8 , who shoots at goal

Common mistakes:
No real understanding between 11 and 8 .
The last pass made by 11 is too slow.

Coaching notes: _____
_____
_____
_____
_____
_____
_____
_____

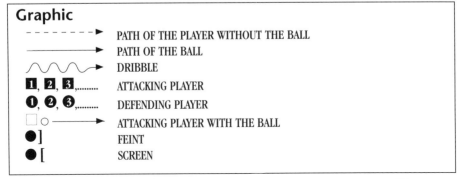

Graphic

- - - - - ▶	PATH OF THE PLAYER WITHOUT THE BALL
──────▶	PATH OF THE BALL
∿∿∿▶	DRIBBLE
1, **2**, **3**,.........	ATTACKING PLAYER
❶, ❷, ❸,.........	DEFENDING PLAYER
☐ ○ ────▶	ATTACKING PLAYER WITH THE BALL
●]	FEINT
●[	SCREEN

Restarting the game at set plays:
Kick-off #5

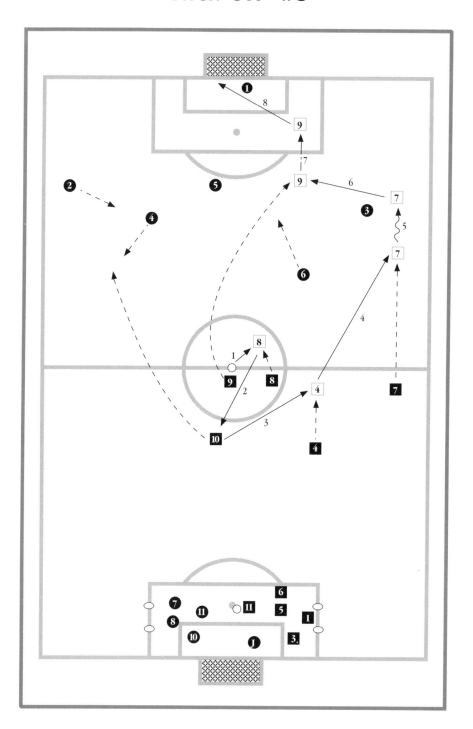

Technical-tactical purposes:
Cooperation in order to score a goal.

Equipment: 2 + 2 + 2 balls; 10 blue + 11 red + 1 white shirts.

Area required: Three-quarter of the field + 1 small-sized field (about 22 x 33 yards).

Coaching methods: Inductive ➡ problem solving.

Description of the offensive situations:
- on one third of the field players practice kick-off exercises, with the consequent possible shot at goal
- a match is played on an adjacent part of the field, or in the free penalty box: 5 v 4 +1 Joker (a player wearing the white shirt), who plays on the team retaining possession of the ball
- count the goals scored during a period of 15 + 15 minutes

Common mistakes:
Difficulties in cooperating, in playing end-to-end combinations and in shooting at goal.

Coaching notes: _____

_____

_____

_____

_____

_____

_____

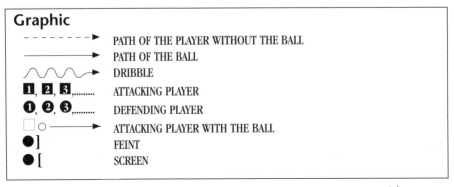

Graphic
- - - - - ►	PATH OF THE PLAYER WITHOUT THE BALL
────►	PATH OF THE BALL
∿∿∿►	DRIBBLE
1, **2**, **3**,........	ATTACKING PLAYER
❶, ❷, ❸,........	DEFENDING PLAYER
□ ○ ────►	ATTACKING PLAYER WITH THE BALL
●]	FEINT
●[	SCREEN

Restarting the game at set plays:
Kick-off #6

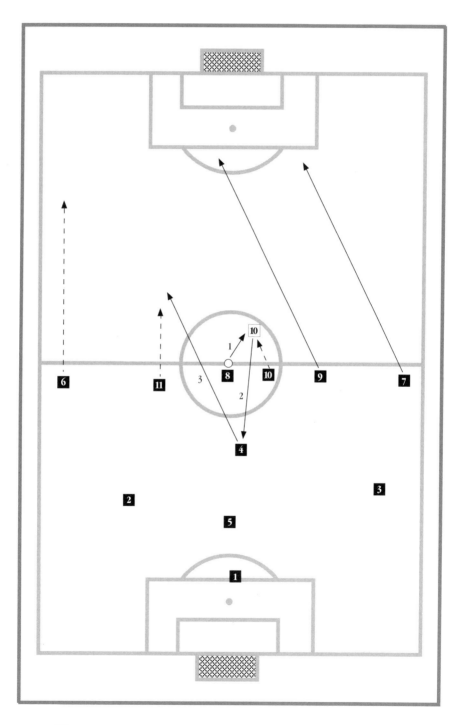

Technical-tactical purposes:
Shadow-play at kick-off.

Equipment: 4 balls; 11 shirts.

Area required: Three-quarters of the field.

Coaching methods: Deductive ➟ prescriptive.

Description of the offensive situations:
- 8 kicks off passing the ball forward to 10, who kicks it back to 4
- 4 makes a diagonal pass to 11, who is running from behind
- 11 heads the ball towards the player 6 or 9.

Common mistakes:
The pass made by 4 to 11 is inaccurate; 6 is not ready when 11 heads the ball towards him.

Coaching notes: _____

_____

_____

_____

_____

_____

_____

_____

_____

_____

Graphic

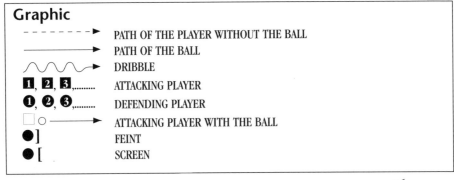

- - - - - - ►   PATH OF THE PLAYER WITHOUT THE BALL
———————►   PATH OF THE BALL
∿∿∿►   DRIBBLE
1, 2, 3..........   ATTACKING PLAYER
❶, ❷, ❸..........   DEFENDING PLAYER
☐ ○ ———►   ATTACKING PLAYER WITH THE BALL
●]   FEINT
●[SCREEN

Restarting the game at set plays:
Goal kick #1

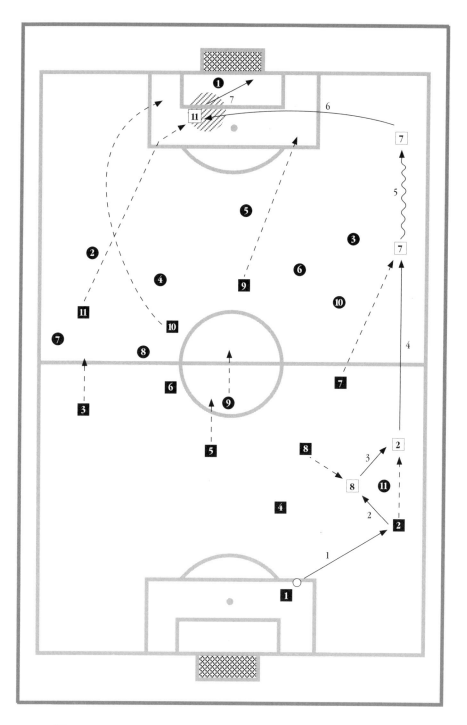

Technical-tactical purposes:
Beginning the offensive combination on the right wing and shooting at goal from the opposite side of the field.

Equipment: 4 balls; 11 + 11 shirts of two different colors.

Area required: Regulation soccer field.

Coaching methods: Inductive ➦ guided discovery.

Description of the offensive situations:
- 1 kicks the ball towards 2 who, pressured by (11), plays the ball to 8 for a give-and-go
- 7 is invited by 2 to gain space towards the opposite goal and receives a deep pass on the right flank of the field. When he gets possession of the ball, he dribbles for some yards and then takes a powerful shot along the line parallel to the 6 yard area, where 11 is running
- 11 volleys the ball, aiming it at the far post.

Common mistakes:
Inaccuracy in the offensive synchronisms between 9 , 10 , 11 .

Coaching notes: _____

_____

_____

_____

_____

_____

_____

Graphic

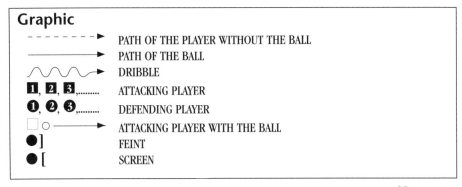

- - - - ➤	PATH OF THE PLAYER WITHOUT THE BALL
⟶➤	PATH OF THE BALL
∿∿∿➤	DRIBBLE
1, **2**, **3**,.........	ATTACKING PLAYER
❶, ❷, ❸,.........	DEFENDING PLAYER
☐ ○ ⟶➤	ATTACKING PLAYER WITH THE BALL
●]	FEINT
● [	SCREEN

Restarting the game at set plays:
Goal kick #2

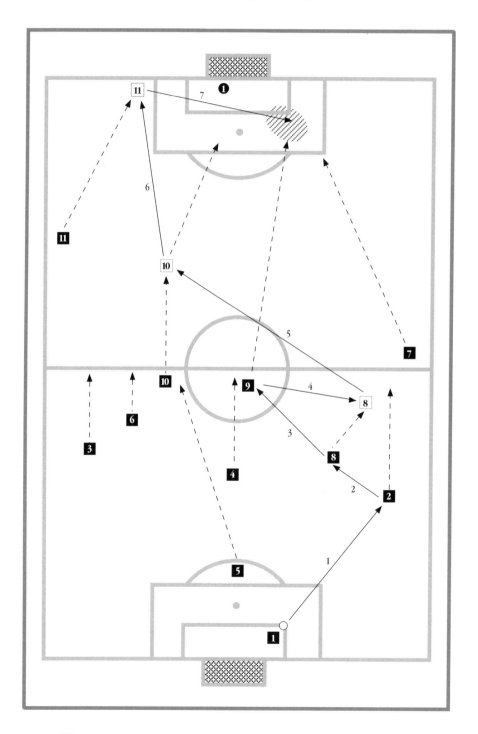

Technical-tactical purposes:
Change of positions and tactical movements in the offensive play.

Equipment: 6 balls; 10 + 2 shirts of different colors.

Area required: Regulation soccer field.

Coaching methods: Deductive ➙ prescriptive.

Description of the offensive situations:
- [1] releases the ball to [2];
- [2] plays the ball to [8], who immediately makes a leftward diagonal pass to [9] and rapidly eludes his opponent to get possession of the ball again
- [8] makes a right-footed pass towards [10].
- [10] has anticipated the penetration of [11] and therefore releases a deep pass for his teammate running forward.
- From the goal-line, [11] crosses to the far corner of the 6 yard box for the penetrating run of [9] or [7].
- [10] runs towards the penalty spot, in order to anticipate the possible clearance by (1).

Common mistakes:
Players do not perform 'give-and-follow' and 'give-and-change-position'.

Coaching notes: _____

_____

_____

_____

_____

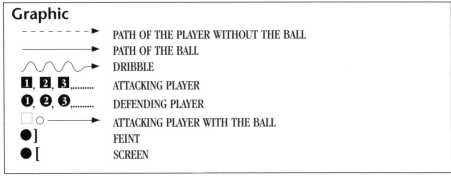

Graphic

- - - - - -►	PATH OF THE PLAYER WITHOUT THE BALL
——————►	PATH OF THE BALL
∿∿∿►	DRIBBLE
1, **2**, **3**,.........	ATTACKING PLAYER
❶, ❷, ❸,.........	DEFENDING PLAYER
□ ○ ————►	ATTACKING PLAYER WITH THE BALL
●]	FEINT
●[	SCREEN

Restarting the game at set plays:
Goal kick #3

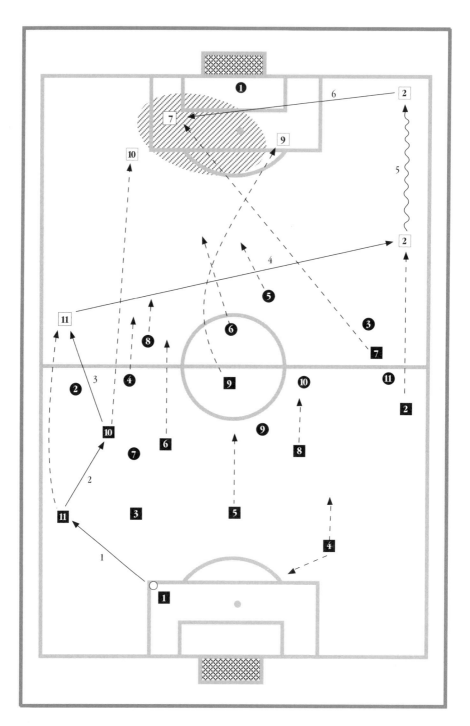

Technical-tactical purposes:
Attack from the left side with a counter pass.

Equipment: 4 balls; 11 + 11 colored shirts.

Area required: Regulation soccer field.

Coaching methods: Deductive ➤ mixed.

Description of the offensive situations:
- the goalkeeper ⛶1 releases the ball to ⛶11, who performs a give-and-go with ⛶10 .
- ⛶11 rapidly makes a long diagonal pass to ⛶2 who, in the meantime, is sprinting on the offensive flank of the field.
- ⛶2 dribbles the ball to the goal-line; then he centers the ball to the far corner of the 6 yard box, where ⛶9 and ⛶7 cross each other.
- ⛶7 stands in the best position to shoot at goal.

Common mistakes:
Difficulties in coordination and accuracy of ⛶11, as well as lack of power in his pass.

Coaching notes: ———————————————————————

———————————————————————————————————

———————————————————————————————————

———————————————————————————————————

———————————————————————————————————

———————————————————————————————————

———————————————————————————————————

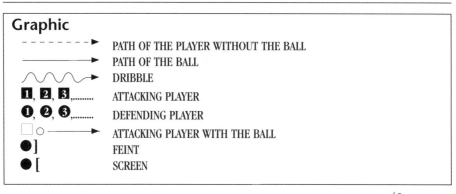

Graphic
------- ►	PATH OF THE PLAYER WITHOUT THE BALL
———————►	PATH OF THE BALL
∿∿∿►	DRIBBLE
1, **2**, **3**,.........	ATTACKING PLAYER
❶, ❷, ❸,.........	DEFENDING PLAYER
☐○ ————►	ATTACKING PLAYER WITH THE BALL
●]	FEINT
●[	SCREEN

Restarting the game at set plays:
Goal kick #4

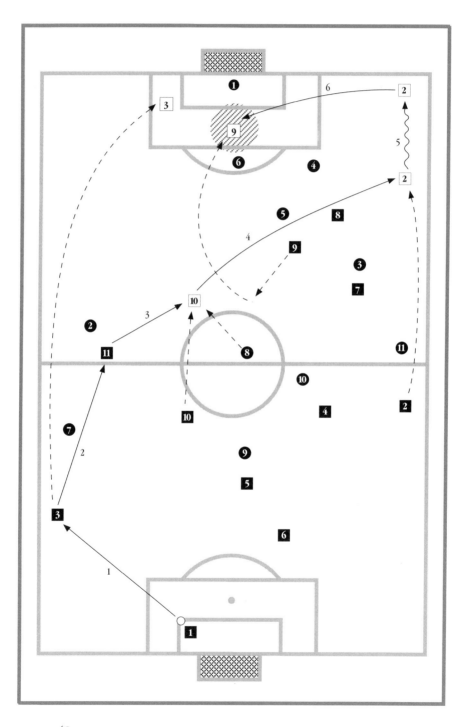

Technical-tactical purposes:
Feint and fake movements in midfield.

Equipment: 6 balls; 11 + 11 shirts of two different colors.

Area required: Regulation soccer field.

Coaching methods: Inductive ➥ guided discovery.

Description of the offensive situations:
- the goalkeeper 1 releases the ball to his teammate 3 ;
  11 moves towards 3 to receive the ball.
- 3 passes to 11 and runs, overlapping his teammate
- 11 centers the ball towards 10 , who is running from behind; he plays a long diagonal pass to 2 , who is moving forward, wide-open on the right wing
- 2 controls the ball and dribbles for some yards, then crosses to 9 ; who shoots at goal, volleying the ball with his right instep.

Common mistakes:
The overlapping runs made by 3 and 2 are not properly covered in the defense; 9 chooses the wrong rhythm of the last three steps, before shooting at goal.

Coaching notes: _____

_____

_____

_____

_____

_____

Graphic

– – – – – ▶	PATH OF THE PLAYER WITHOUT THE BALL
──────▶	PATH OF THE BALL
∿∿∿▶	DRIBBLE
1, **2**, **3**,.........	ATTACKING PLAYER
❶, ❷, ❸,.........	DEFENDING PLAYER
□ ○ ──▶	ATTACKING PLAYER WITH THE BALL
●]	FEINT
● [	SCREEN

Restarting the game at set plays:
Goal kick #5

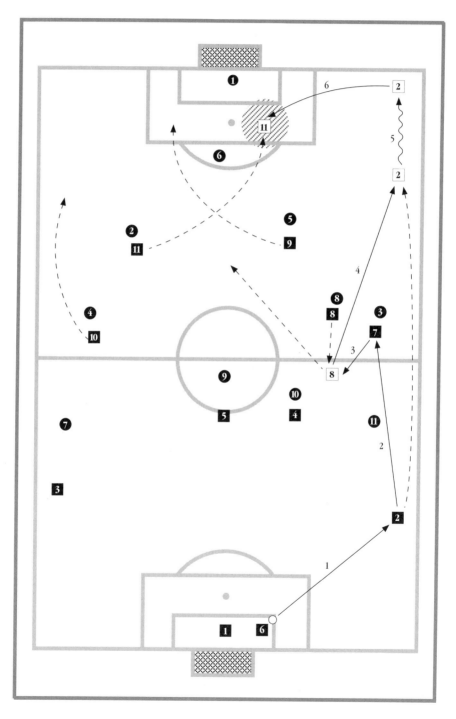

Technical-tactical purposes:
Eluding the opponents' marking and performing central cross-over plays.

Equipment: 3 + 3 balls; 11 + 11 shirts of two different colors.

Area required: Regulation soccer field.

Coaching methods: Inductive ➤➤ problem solving.

Description of the offensive situations:
- The defender 6 directs the goal kick towards 2 ;
- 2 , eluding the marking of ⑪ , finds the space for a deep pass to 7 ;
- he spots his teammate 8 , unmarked, and plays the ball to him.
- In the meantime, 2 sprints in an overlapping run to receive a deep pass made by 8 ;
- 2 controls the ball and dribbles for some yards; then he plays the ball towards 11 .
- After performing a cross-over run with 9 , 11 can finally shoot at goal.

Common mistakes:
The overlap, the control and the dribble performed by 2 are not synchronized with the cross-over runs of 9 and 11 .

Coaching notes: _____

_____

_____

_____

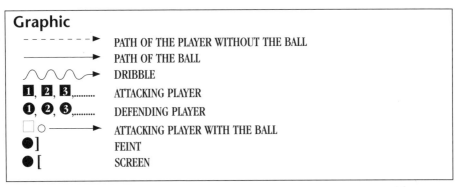

Graphic

– – – – – ▶	PATH OF THE PLAYER WITHOUT THE BALL
——————▶	PATH OF THE BALL
∿∿∿∿▶	DRIBBLE
1, **2**, **3**,........	ATTACKING PLAYER
❶, ❷, ❸,........	DEFENDING PLAYER
☐ ○ ——▶	ATTACKING PLAYER WITH THE BALL
●]	FEINT
● [	SCREEN

Restarting the game at set plays:
Goal kick #6

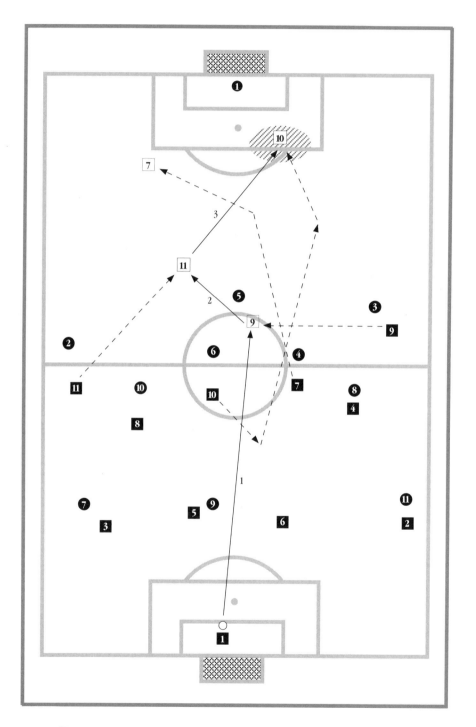

Technical-tactical purposes:
Performing cross-over plays and eluding the opponents' marking at midfield.

Equipment: 6 balls; 11 + 11 shirts of two different colors.

Area required: Regulation soccer field.

Coaching methods: Inductive ➤ free exploration.

Description of the offensive situations:
- the goalkeeper 1 drop kicks the ball towards the center circle
- the player 9 is a good header of the ball; he sprints from the right flank of the field and, when the ball is arriving in the center circle, he moves rapidly to meet it, jumps and heads the ball, aiming it towards 11, who is running forward from the left side
- in the meantime, 7 and 10 get into the offensive action.
- 11 wins possession of the ball and, after a quick control, plays it to 10 in the line of his run.
- 10 and 7 elude the opponents' marking through a cross-over play.

Common mistakes: Timing of runs, either too early or too late:

Coaching notes: _____
_____
_____
_____
_____
_____

Graphic

- - - - - - ▶	PATH OF THE PLAYER WITHOUT THE BALL
────────▶	PATH OF THE BALL
∿∿∿∿▶	DRIBBLE
1, **2**, **3**,........	ATTACKING PLAYER
❶, ❷, ❸,........	DEFENDING PLAYER
☐ ○ ────▶	ATTACKING PLAYER WITH THE BALL
●]	FEINT
● [	SCREEN

Restarting the game at set plays:
Goal kick #7

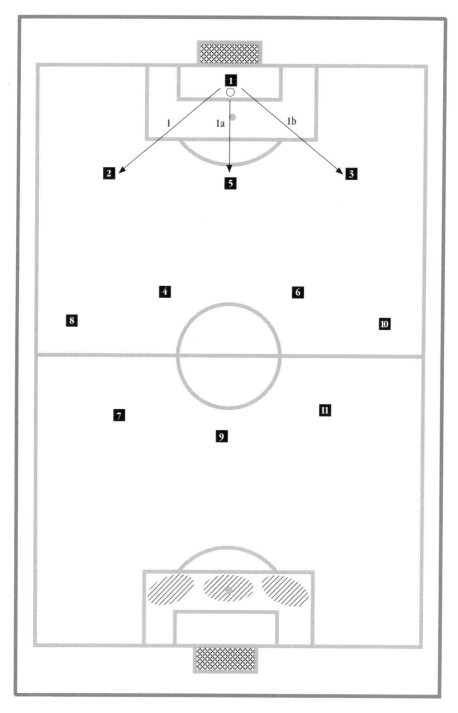

Technical-tactical purposes:
Offensive action aimed at spreading out the team in order to force the opponents to leave free spaces to exploit.

Equipment: Supply of Balls, 11 players.

Area required: Regulation soccer field.

Coaching methods: Inductive ➻ problem solving.

Description of the offensive situations:
- there are different solutions for the goalkeeper to restart the game, since ⟦2⟧, ⟦3⟧, ⟦5⟧ position so as to receive the ball.
- ⟦8⟧ and ⟦10⟧ are on their respective wings;
- ⟦4⟧ and ⟦6⟧ are ready to receive the ball, which means that they are in the right positions to support the three defenders.
- ⟦7⟧ occupies the center-right space;
- ⟦11⟧ occupies the center-left area;
- ⟦9⟧ stands in the central space.

Common mistakes: _____
_____
_____
_____

Coaching notes: _____
_____
_____
_____
_____

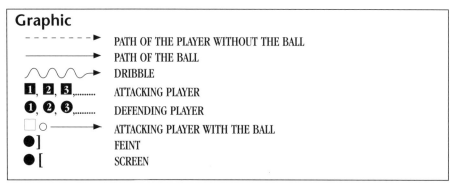

Graphic

- - - - - - ➤	PATH OF THE PLAYER WITHOUT THE BALL
———➤	PATH OF THE BALL
∿∿∿➤	DRIBBLE
1, **2**, **3**,.........	ATTACKING PLAYER
❶, ❷, ❸,.........	DEFENDING PLAYER
☐ ○ ———➤	ATTACKING PLAYER WITH THE BALL
●]	FEINT
● [	SCREEN

Restarting the game at set plays:
Goal kick #8

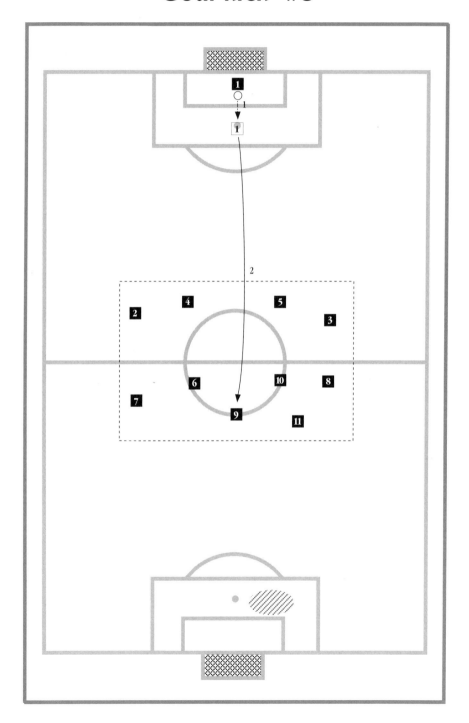

Technical-tactical purposes:
Compactness of the team in a given space.

Equipment: Supply of Balls, 11 players.

Area required: Regulation soccer field.

Coaching methods: Inductive ➡ free exploration.

Description of the offensive situations:
- while the goalkeeper is about to take the goal kick, all the team shall compact in midfield; in this way, the players are in the best position to win the ball.
- ⬚9 is the central pivot and the point of reference for all the team.

Common mistakes: Players do not move quickly enough into the compact area:

Coaching notes: —————————————————————

_____

_____

_____

_____

_____

_____

_____

_____

_____

Graphic
- - - - - - -▶ PATH OF THE PLAYER WITHOUT THE BALL
————————▶ PATH OF THE BALL
〰〰〰▶ DRIBBLE
1, 2, 3,......... ATTACKING PLAYER
❶, ❷, ❸,......... DEFENDING PLAYER
☐○————▶ ATTACKING PLAYER WITH THE BALL
●] FEINT
●[SCREEN

Restarting the game at set plays:
Goal kick #9

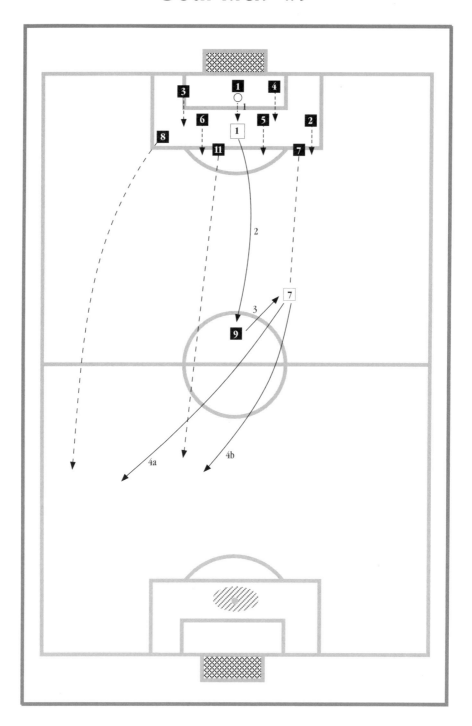

Technical-tactical purposes:
Shifting directly from a corner kick to the offensive phase.
Counter attack.

Equipment: Supply of balls, 11 players.

Area required: Regulation soccer field.

Coaching methods: Deductive ➤➤ assigning tasks.

Description of the offensive situations:
- 1 gets possession of the ball by intercepting a high cross from the corner kick.
- 1 moves forward dribbling for some yards; then he passes to the unmarked 9 , using an overarm throw.
- 9 waits for the vertical penetration of 7 , while, in the meantime, 8 and 11 sprint forward to take part in the offensive action.
- All the other players rapidly push up towards the midfield, to support the offensive play.

Common mistakes: Players do not move forward and wide as soon as the goalkeeper intercepts the ball.

Coaching notes: _____

_____

_____

_____

_____

_____

Graphic

- - - - - - ►	PATH OF THE PLAYER WITHOUT THE BALL
————►	PATH OF THE BALL
∿∿∿►	DRIBBLE
1, **2**, **3**,.........	ATTACKING PLAYER
❶, **❷**, **❸**,.........	DEFENDING PLAYER
☐ ○ ————►	ATTACKING PLAYER WITH THE BALL
●]	FEINT
●[	SCREEN

Restarting the game at set plays:
Corner kick #1

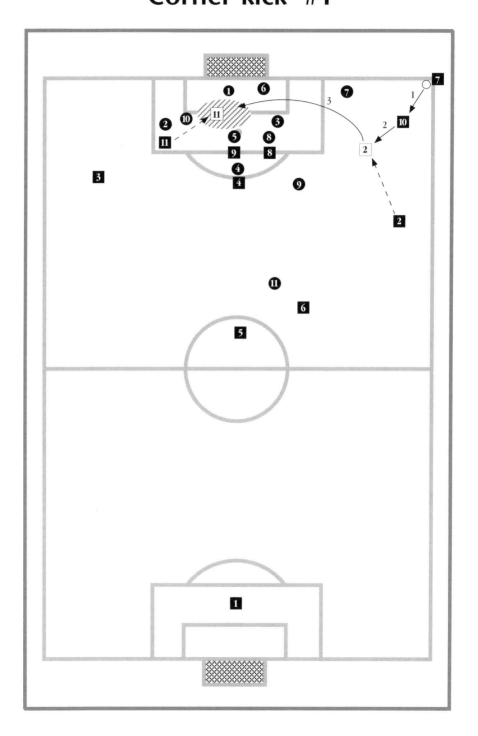

Technical-tactical purposes:
Corner kick from the right: 2 back passes and an inswinging cross.

Equipment: 4 balls; 11 + 11 shirts of two different colors.

Area required: Half of the field and a full-sized goal.

Coaching methods: Deductive ➤➤ prescriptive.

Description of the offensive situations:
- the forward 7 takes the corner, kicking the ball to his teammate 10 who, in turn, passes the ball to 2 , who is running from behind.
- 2 immediately crosses the ball towards the far corner of the 6 yard box, where 11 is sprinting, surprising all his opponents.

Common mistakes:
Lack of synchronism (speed and accuracy) between 7 , 10 , 2 , 11 .

Coaching notes: _____

_____

_____

_____

_____

_____

_____

_____

_____

_____

Graphic

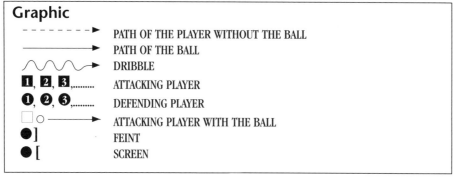

- - - - - - -►	PATH OF THE PLAYER WITHOUT THE BALL
————►	PATH OF THE BALL
∿∿∿►	DRIBBLE
1, **2**, **3**,..........	ATTACKING PLAYER
❶, **❷**, **❸**,..........	DEFENDING PLAYER
□ ○ ————►	ATTACKING PLAYER WITH THE BALL
●]	FEINT
●[	SCREEN

Restarting the game at set plays:
Corner kick #2

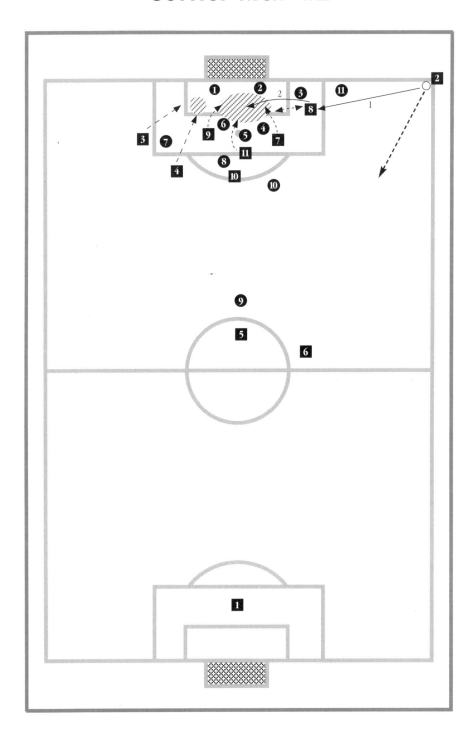

Technical-tactical purposes:
Corner kick and faking movements within the penalty box.

Equipment: 3 + 3 balls; 11 + 11 shirts of two different colors.

Area required: Regulation soccer field.

Coaching methods: Inductive ➡ problem solving.

Description of the offensive situations:
- the player 8 fakes to move towards the 6 yard box, then sprints to meet the cross made by his teammate 2 .
- 8 heads the crossed ball (impact with the upper forehead) and directs it towards the line of the goal area, where, after performing some fakes, 9 , 11 , 7 can respectively advance
- if 8 heads the ball in such a way that its path is too long, 3 and 4 are ready to take part in the action to meet the ball
- after taking the corner, 2 quickly returns towards the midfield area

Common mistakes:
8 does not head the ball in the proper way; 9 , 11 , 7 cut to the same place.

Coaching notes: _____

_____

_____

_____

_____

_____

Graphic

- - - - - - ➤	PATH OF THE PLAYER WITHOUT THE BALL
———————➤	PATH OF THE BALL
∿∿∿➤	DRIBBLE
1, **2**, **3**,.........	ATTACKING PLAYER
❶, ❷, ❸,.........	DEFENDING PLAYER
▢ ○ ———➤	ATTACKING PLAYER WITH THE BALL
●]	FEINT
●[	SCREEN

Restarting the game at set plays:
Corner kick #3

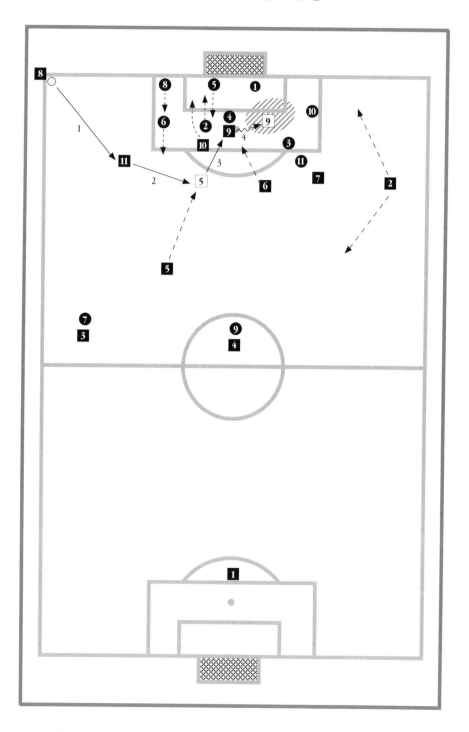

Technical-tactical purposes:
Corner kick from the left and pass towards the corner of the penalty area.

Equipment: 3 + 3 balls; 11 + 11 shirts of two different colors.

Area required: Regulation soccer field.

Coaching methods: Deductive ➤➤ mixed.

Description of the offensive situations:
- the player $\boxed{8}$, who takes the corner kick from the left, delivers the ball to $\boxed{11}$, at the near corner of the penalty area
- $\boxed{11}$ immediately plays the ball into the path of his teammate $\boxed{5}$, who directly passes it to $\boxed{9}$.
- $\boxed{9}$ controls the ball, dribbles and then shoots at goal.

Common mistakes:
$\boxed{6}$ impedes the movement of $\boxed{9}$, instead of creating space around him.

Coaching notes: ───────────────────────────────

───

───

───

───

───

───

───

Graphic

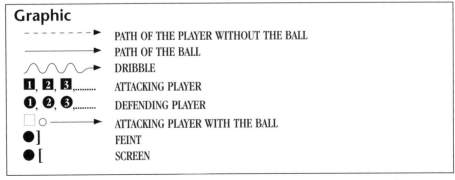

- - - - - ▶	PATH OF THE PLAYER WITHOUT THE BALL
────────▶	PATH OF THE BALL
∿∿∿▶	DRIBBLE
1, **2**, **3**,.........	ATTACKING PLAYER
❶, ❷, ❸,.........	DEFENDING PLAYER
□ ○ ────▶	ATTACKING PLAYER WITH THE BALL
●]	FEINT
●[	SCREEN

Restarting the game at set plays:
Corner kick #4

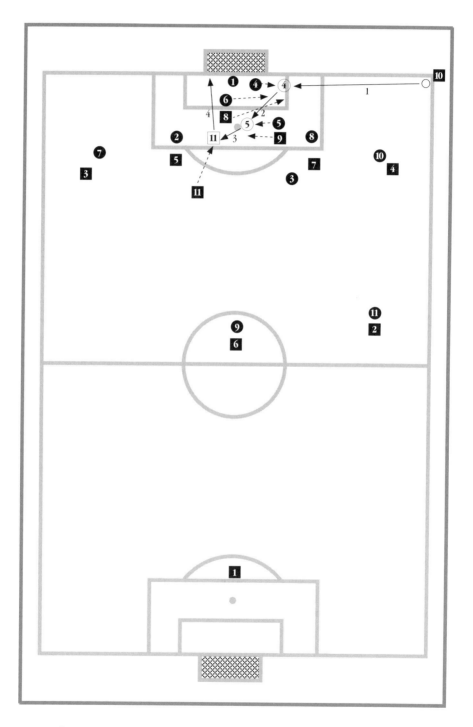

Technical-tactical purposes:
Volley shot taken with the right instep.

Equipment: 2 + 2 balls.

Area required: Regulation soccer field.

Coaching methods: Inductive ➡ free exploration.

Description of the offensive situations:
- the forward 10 passes the ball towards the running 8.
- the defender ④ anticipates the pass, intercepts and heads the ball towards his teammate ⑤ who, challenged by 9, can do nothing but make an unintentional pass to 11.
- 11 tries to coordinate in the best way so as to shoot at goal with his right instep.

Common mistakes:
10 kicks the ball too early compared to the speed of 8.
④ should have headed the ball outside the penalty box

Coaching notes: _____

_____

_____

_____

_____

_____

_____

_____

_____

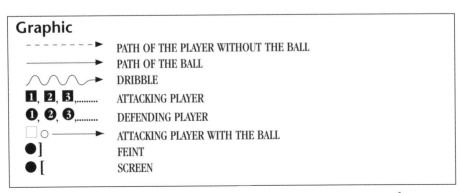

Graphic

- - - - - ➤	PATH OF THE PLAYER WITHOUT THE BALL
⎯⎯⎯➤	PATH OF THE BALL
∿∿∿➤	DRIBBLE
1, **2**, **3**,.........	ATTACKING PLAYER
❶, **❷**, **❸**,.........	DEFENDING PLAYER
☐○ ⎯⎯➤	ATTACKING PLAYER WITH THE BALL
●]	FEINT
●[	SCREEN

Restarting the game at set plays:
Corner kick #5

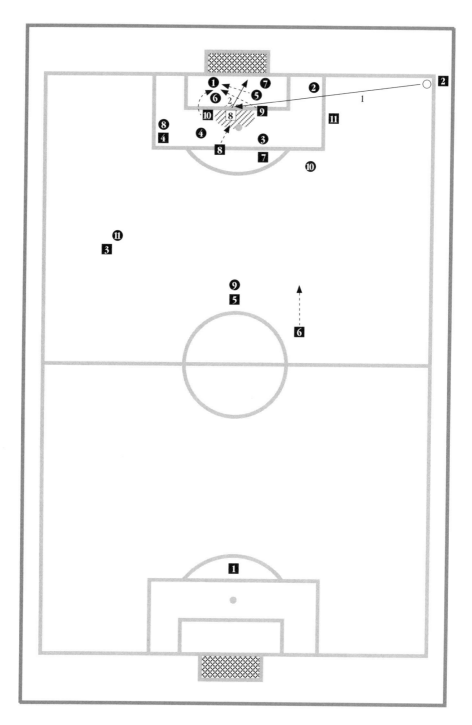

Technical-tactical purposes:
Screen the goalkeeper.

Equipment: 3 + 3 balls; 11 + 11 shirts of two different colors.

Area required: Regulation soccer field.

Coaching methods: Deductive ➤ assigning tasks.

Description of the offensive situations:
- the player 2 takes the corner kick
- before the corner is taken, 9 and 10 move towards the goalkeeper (1) to perform the screen.
- 2 delivers the ball towards the edge of the 6 yard area, where 8 is sprinting to shoot at goal with a volley.

Common mistakes:
 9 and 10 perform the screen too early or too late.

Coaching notes: _____

_____

_____

_____

_____

_____

_____

_____

_____

_____

Graphic

– – – – – – ►	PATH OF THE PLAYER WITHOUT THE BALL
───────►	PATH OF THE BALL
∿∿∿►	DRIBBLE
1, **2**, **3**,.........	ATTACKING PLAYER
❶, ❷, ❸,.........	DEFENDING PLAYER
☐ ○ ──────►	ATTACKING PLAYER WITH THE BALL
●]	FEINT
● [	SCREEN

Restarting the game at set plays:
Corner kick #6

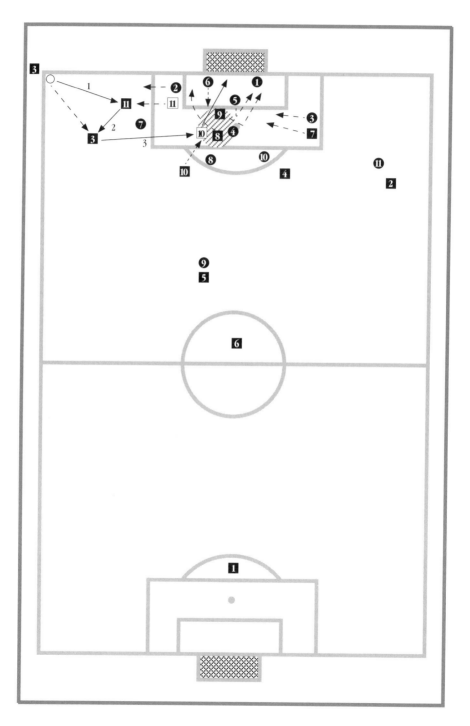

Technical-tactical purposes:
Cross-over play within the penalty box at a corner kick from the left.

Equipment: Supply of balls; 11 + 11 shirts of two different colors.

Area required: Regulation soccer field.

Coaching methods: Inductive ➤➤ problem solving.

Description of the offensive situations:
- the player ⬚3 takes the corner kick. He makes a ground pass towards ⬚11, who is rapidly moving to meet the ball
- after controlling the ball, ⬚11 passes it backward to ⬚3 who is moving to take part in the organization of the offensive play
- in the meantime, ⬚9 and ⬚8 perform a cross-over play within the penalty box, running respectively towards the two opposite posts,
- in this way, there is room for ⬚10 to shoot at goal freely from the cross of ⬚3 .

Common mistakes:
⬚9 and ⬚8 perform the cross-over play too early, allowing the defense to recover.

Coaching notes: _____
_____
_____
_____
_____
_____
_____

Graphic

- - - - - ►	PATH OF THE PLAYER WITHOUT THE BALL
————►	PATH OF THE BALL
∿∿∿►	DRIBBLE
1, **2**, **3**,........	ATTACKING PLAYER
❶, ❷, ❸,........	DEFENDING PLAYER
⬚ ○ ————►	ATTACKING PLAYER WITH THE BALL
●]	FEINT
● [	SCREEN

Restarting the game at set plays:
Corner kick #7

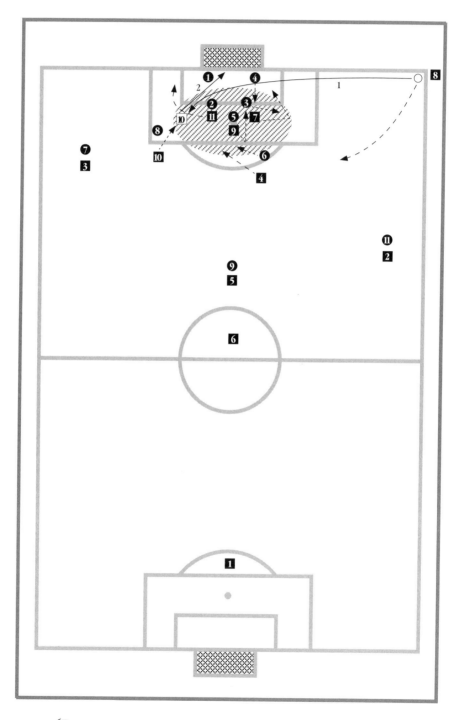

Technical-tactical purposes:
Eluding the opponents' marking through an 'explosive' movement within the penalty area.

Equipment: Supply of balls; 11 + 11 shirts of two different colors.

Area required: Half a soccer field.

Coaching methods: Inductive ➜ free exploration.

Description of the offensive situations:
- 8 takes the corner kick with the instep, aiming the ball towards the far angle of the 6 yard box.
- 11, 9, 7 intentionally engage in a scrimmage around the penalty spot.
- At a conventional signal, they 'burst', sprinting in three different directions, previously decided; in this way, they create a free lane for the running 10 who shoots at goal.

Common mistakes:
8 takes an inaccurate corner kick, 10 does not move at the right moment.

Coaching notes: _____

_____

_____

_____

_____

_____

_____

_____

_____

_____

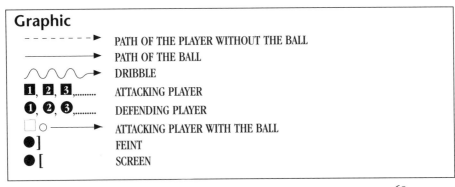

Graphic

- - - - - - - ►	PATH OF THE PLAYER WITHOUT THE BALL
─────────►	PATH OF THE BALL
∿∿∿►	DRIBBLE
1, **2**, **3**,.........	ATTACKING PLAYER
❶, ❷, ❸,.........	DEFENDING PLAYER
□ o ─────►	ATTACKING PLAYER WITH THE BALL
●]	FEINT
● [	SCREEN

Restarting the game at set plays:
Corner kick #8

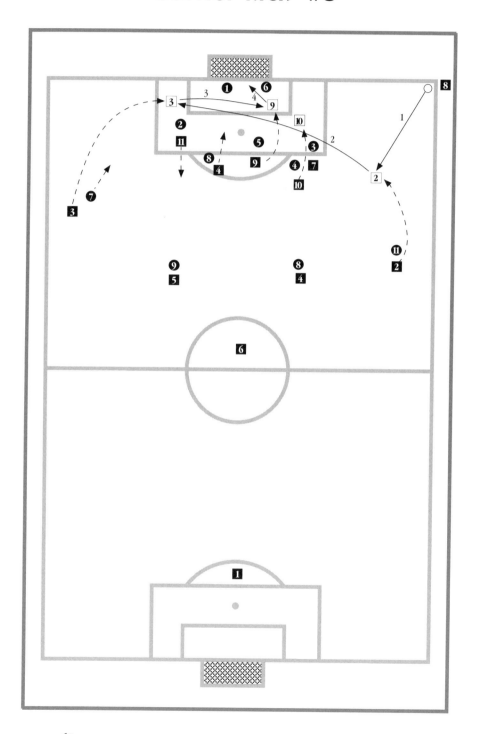

Technical-tactical purposes:
Corner kick with the two full-backs taking part in the offensive action.

Equipment: Supply of Balls, 11 + 11 players.

Area required: Half of soccer field.

Coaching methods: Inductive ➤➤ free exploration.

Description of the offensive situations:
- [8] plays the ball to the running [2], who directly kicks it with the right instep for the dynamic penetration of [3].
- [3] plays the ball towards the 6 yard box, with an inswerve for his teammate [9], who can easily shoot at goal.

Common mistakes: Last pass is made too deep, allowing the goalkeeper to intercept.

Coaching notes:_____
_____
_____
_____
_____
_____
_____
_____
_____
_____
_____

Graphic

– – – – – ➤	PATH OF THE PLAYER WITHOUT THE BALL
———➤	PATH OF THE BALL
∿∿∿➤	DRIBBLE
1, **2**, **3**,.........	ATTACKING PLAYER
❶, **❷**, **❸**,.........	DEFENDING PLAYER
☐ ○ ———➤	ATTACKING PLAYER WITH THE BALL
●]	FEINT
● [	SCREEN

Restarting the game at set plays:
Corner kick #9

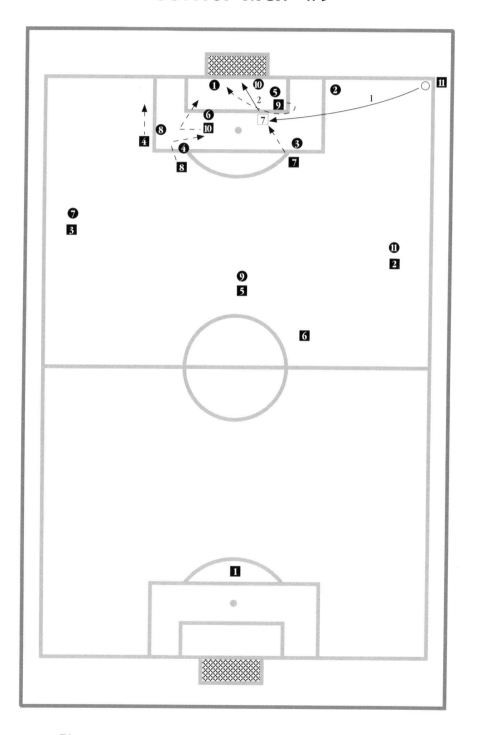

Technical-tactical purposes:
Clearing the space at the near post.

Equipment: Supply of balls, 11 + 11 players.

Area required: Half of soccer field.

Coaching methods: Inductive ➤ problem solving.

Description of the offensive situations:
- while 11 is taking a short run before kicking the corner,
- 9 pretends to run upward, but he then moves towards the opposing goalkeeper.
- 9 and 10 clear the space within the penalty box, so as to help the useful penetration of 7 from behind,
- 7 runs forward to shoot at goal the cross made by 11.

Common mistakes: 9 's feint is too slow, clogging the space need-ed for 7 to shoot at goal.

Coaching notes: _____

_____

_____

_____

_____

_____

_____

_____

_____

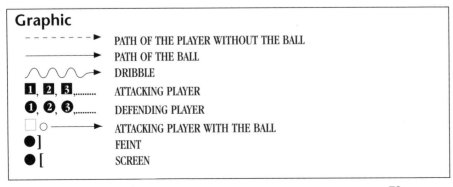

Graphic

- - - - - - ➤	PATH OF THE PLAYER WITHOUT THE BALL
⟶	PATH OF THE BALL
∿∿∿➤	DRIBBLE
1, **2**, **3**,........	ATTACKING PLAYER
❶, ❷, ❸,........	DEFENDING PLAYER
☐ ○ ⟶	ATTACKING PLAYER WITH THE BALL
●]	FEINT
●[	SCREEN

Restarting the game at set plays:
Corner kick #10

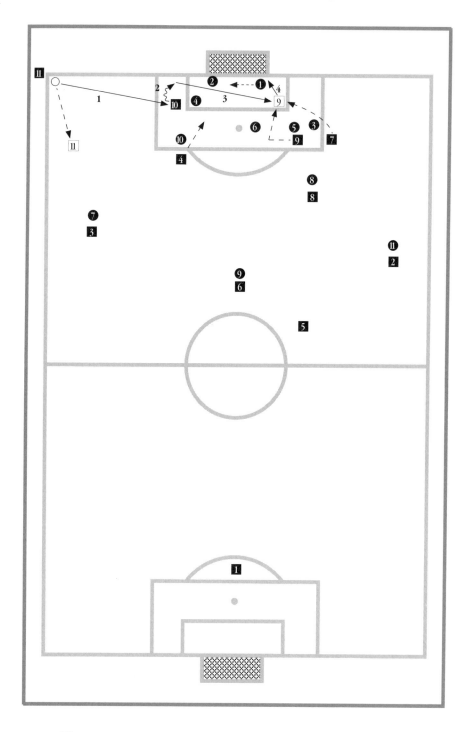

Technical-tactical purposes:
Corner kick with supporting play.

Equipment: Supply of balls, 11 + 11 players.

Area required: Half of soccer field.

Coaching methods: Inductive ➤ problem solving

Description of the offensive situations:
- 11 pretends to cross the ball towards the penalty area, but he then gives a pass to the running 10.
- after passing the ball to 10, 11 runs towards the left angle of the 18 yard box.
- 10 pretends to pass the ball back to 11, but, with a change of pace, he rapidly dribbles the ball up to the goal line; from this position, he gives a cross towards the far post.
- 9 and 7 pretend to move off the play, but they suddenly sprint towards the goal area.
- 9 is likely to meet the ball first so that he can shoot at goal at the near post.

Common mistakes: 9 and/or 7 fail to 'sell' their feints.

Coaching notes: _____

_____

_____

_____

_____

_____

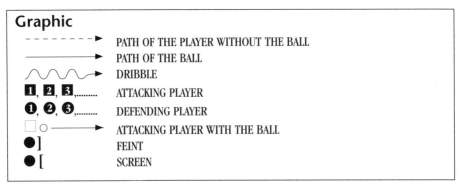

Graphic
- - - - - ➤	PATH OF THE PLAYER WITHOUT THE BALL
———➤	PATH OF THE BALL
∿∿∿➤	DRIBBLE
1, 2, 3,.........	ATTACKING PLAYER
❶, ❷, ❸,.........	DEFENDING PLAYER
□ ○ ———➤	ATTACKING PLAYER WITH THE BALL
●]	FEINT
●[	SCREEN

Restarting the game at set plays:
Corner kick #11

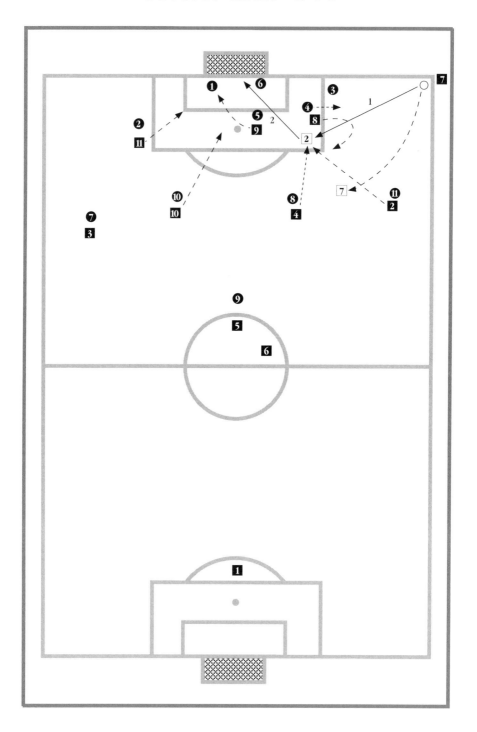

Technical-tactical purposes:
Corner kick.

Equipment: Supply of balls, 11 + 11 players.

Area required: Half of soccer field.

Coaching methods: Inductive ➻ problem solving.

Description of the offensive situations:
- the forward ⎡7⎤ takes the corner kick aiming the ball at the corner of the penalty box.
- ⎡4⎤ and ⎡2⎤ rapidly run in that direction to cooperate in the organization of the offensive play.
- ⎡4⎤ leaves the ball to ⎡2⎤, who directly shoots at goal, trying to direct the ball towards the near post.

Common mistakes: Inaccuracy in the timing between ⎡2⎤ and ⎡4⎤.

Coaching notes: _____

_____

_____

_____

_____

_____

_____

_____

_____

_____

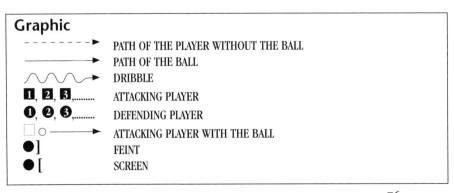

Graphic

- - - - - ►	PATH OF THE PLAYER WITHOUT THE BALL
──────►	PATH OF THE BALL
∿∿∿►	DRIBBLE
1, **2**, **3**,.........	ATTACKING PLAYER
❶, ❷, ❸,.........	DEFENDING PLAYER
☐ ○ ──────►	ATTACKING PLAYER WITH THE BALL
●]	FEINT
●[	SCREEN

Restarting the game at set plays:
Corner kick #12

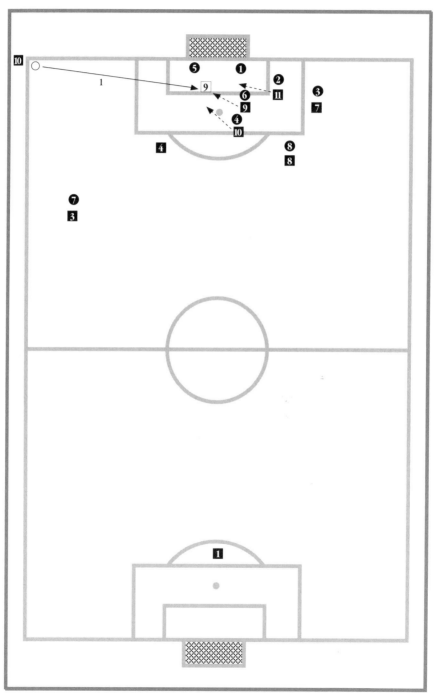

Technical-tactical purposes:
Lineup behind the penalty spot.

Equipment: Supply of balls, 8 + 8 players.

Area required: Half a soccer field.

Coaching methods: Inductive ➡ guided discovery.

Description of the offensive situations:
- 10 kicks the ball slightly beyond the left angle of the goal area.
- His teammates 9 , 10 , 11 sprint from their positions behind the penalty spot.
- 9 is first to the ball and shoots at goal.

Common mistakes: 9 , 10 , and 11 fail to communicate who will take the shot.

Coaching notes: ──────────────────────────

──

──

──

──

──

──

──

──

──

Graphic

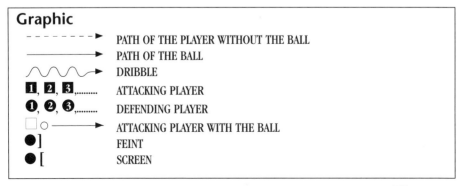

- - - - - - - ➤   PATH OF THE PLAYER WITHOUT THE BALL
─────────➤   PATH OF THE BALL
〰〰〰➤   DRIBBLE
1, **2**, **3**,..........   ATTACKING PLAYER
❶, **❷**, **❸**,..........   DEFENDING PLAYER
□ ○ ─────➤   ATTACKING PLAYER WITH THE BALL
●]   FEINT
● [SCREEN

Restarting the game at set plays:
Corner kick #13

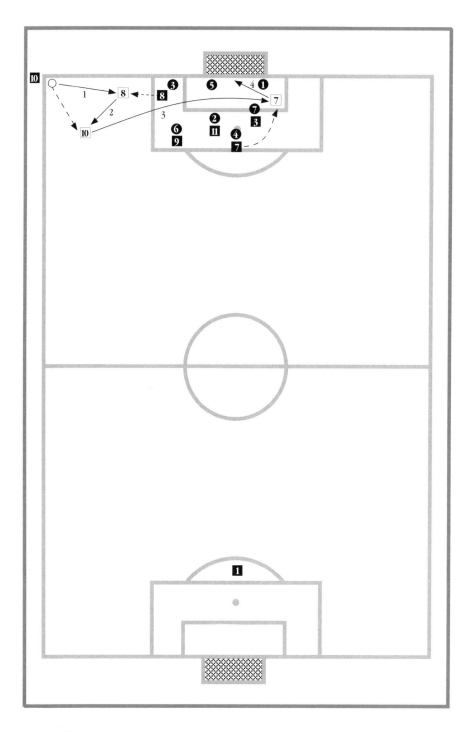

Technical-tactical purposes:
Wall-passing at a corner kick from the left.

Equipment: Supply of balls, 11 + 11.

Area required: Half of the field.

Coaching methods: Inductive ➡ problem solving.

Description of the offensive situations:
- 10 passes the ball to his teammate 8, who is running towards him to meet the ball.
- after playing the ball, 10 runs towards the left angle of the 18 yard box.
- 8 passes the ball to 10, on the line of his run;
- after controlling the ball, 10 kicks it with the outside of his right foot towards the right angle of the 6 yard box, where 7 is running to shoot at goal.

Common mistakes: Cross is made too near the goal.

Coaching notes: —————————————————————

Graphic

- - - - ➤	PATH OF THE PLAYER WITHOUT THE BALL
——➤	PATH OF THE BALL
∿∿∿➤	DRIBBLE
1, 2, 3,.........	ATTACKING PLAYER
❶, ❷, ❸,.........	DEFENDING PLAYER
☐○——➤	ATTACKING PLAYER WITH THE BALL
●]	FEINT
●[	SCREEN

Restarting the game at set plays:
Corner kick #14

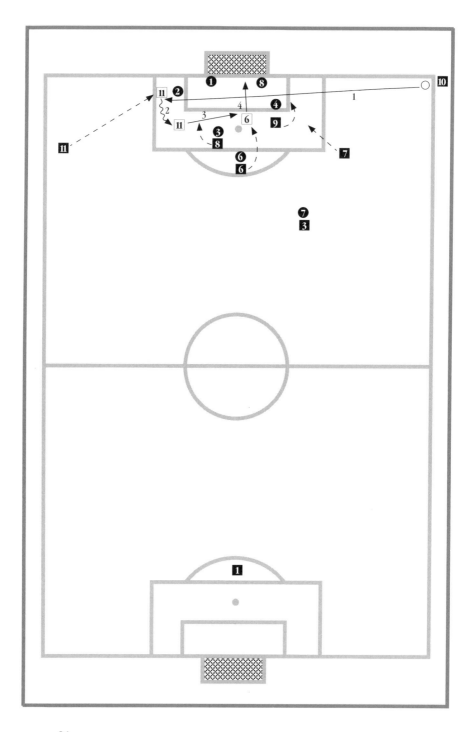

Technical-tactical purposes:
Corner kick towards the far line of the goal area.

Equipment: Supply of balls, 11 + 11.

Area required: Half of the field.

Coaching methods: Inductive ➤➤ problem solving.

Description of the offensive situations:
- [10] makes a long pass towards [11], who is rapidly sprinting from the left wing to take part in the offensive action within the penalty box.
- [11] controls the ball, dribbles for some yards and then kicks it with the instep on the line of the running [6],
- who shoots at goal with his left foot.

Common mistakes: The final pass lacks power and/or accuracy.

Coaching notes: _____

_____

_____

_____

_____

_____

_____

_____

_____

Graphic

- - - - - - ►	PATH OF THE PLAYER WITHOUT THE BALL
―――――►	PATH OF THE BALL
∿∿∿►	DRIBBLE
1, **2**, **3**,.........	ATTACKING PLAYER
❶, ❷, ❸,.........	DEFENDING PLAYER
☐ ○ ―――►	ATTACKING PLAYER WITH THE BALL
●]	FEINT
●[	SCREEN

Restarting the game at set plays:
Corner kick #15

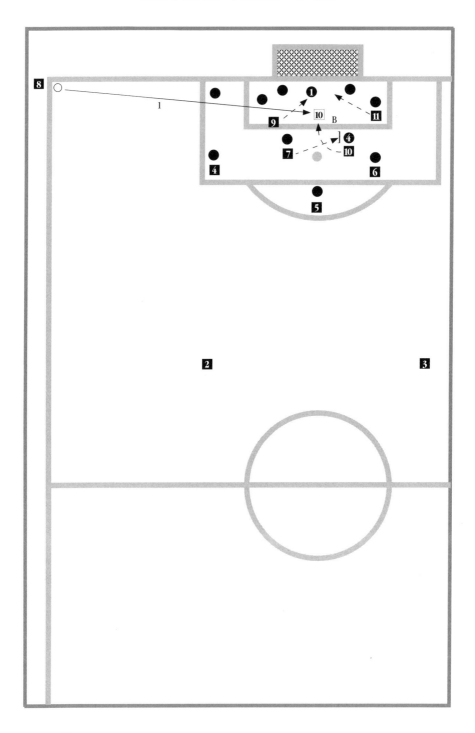

Technical-tactical purposes:
Clearing the space for a teammate within the goal area by means of a screen.

Equipment: Supply of balls, 11+ 11 players.

Area required: Half of soccer field.

Coaching methods: Deductive ➼ assigned tasks.

Description of the offensive situations:
- ⎡8⎤ kicks with the instep, directing the ball towards the mid-goal area.
- ⎡9⎤ and ⎡11⎤ run towards the goalkeeper in order to obstruct his movements.
- with a body swerve ⎡7⎤ sprints towards ④ to perform the screen.
- exploiting the screen on ④, ⎡10⎤ can freely move along the central lane and shoot at goal.
- ⎡4⎤, ⎡5⎤, ⎡6⎤ are ready to intervene in case of a possible mistake or clearance.

Common mistakes: In performing the screens there is a tendency to foul.

Coaching notes: _____

_____

_____

_____

_____

_____

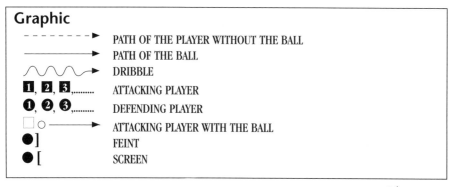

Graphic
– – – – – – ▶	PATH OF THE PLAYER WITHOUT THE BALL
─────────▶	PATH OF THE BALL
∿∿∿∿▶	DRIBBLE
1, **2**, **3**,.........	ATTACKING PLAYER
❶, ❷, ❸,.........	DEFENDING PLAYER
☐ ○ ─────▶	ATTACKING PLAYER WITH THE BALL
●]	FEINT
●[	SCREEN

Restarting the game at set plays:
Corner kick #16

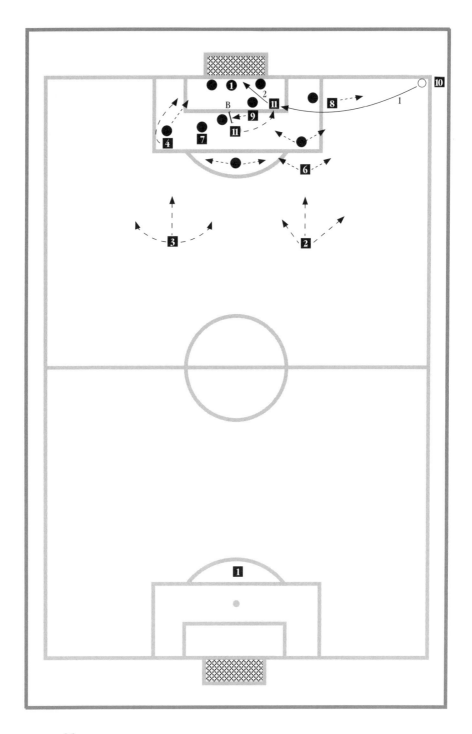

Technical-tactical purposes:

Clearing the space for a teammate at the near post, by means of a screen. 10 signals which corner kick variation he is going to play through a sign previously agreed upon (e.g. ground pass, near post or far post etc.).

Equipment: Supply of balls, 11+ 11 players.

Area required: Half of soccer field.

Coaching methods: Deductive ➵ assigned tasks.

Description of the offensive situations:
- 10 kicks the ball towards the near post within the goal area.
- 8 moves towards 10 , in order to draw his opponent away from the penalty box.
- 9 performs the screen on the opponent of 11 .
- Thanks to the screen performed by his teammate, 11 can easily move to win the ball and shoot at goal.
- 7 and 4 are ready to intervene from the left.

Common mistakes: All the attacking players do not know which corner variation is being played.

Coaching notes: _____

_____

_____

_____

_____

_____

_____

Graphic

– – – – – – ▶	PATH OF THE PLAYER WITHOUT THE BALL
───────▶	PATH OF THE BALL
∿∿∿▶	DRIBBLE
1, **2**, **3**,.........	ATTACKING PLAYER
❶, ❷, ❸,.........	DEFENDING PLAYER
☐ ○ ───▶	ATTACKING PLAYER WITH THE BALL
●]	FEINT
●[	SCREEN

Restarting the game at set plays:
Corner kick #17

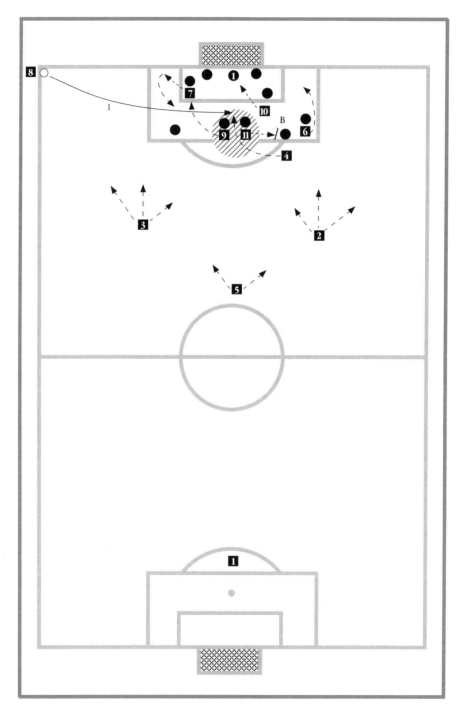

Technical-tactical purposes:

Clearing the space for a teammate near the penalty spot, by means of a screen.

Sign previously agreed upon: 8 stands with his hands on his hips.

Equipment: Supply of balls, 11+ 11 players.

Area required: Half of soccer field.

Coaching methods: Deductive ➡ assigned tasks.

Description of the offensive situations:

- 8 kicks with the instep and directs the ball towards 4 , on the penalty spot.
- 11 moves towards the defender of 4 in order to obstruct him.
- 9 draws his defender off his position.
- After performing some faking movements, 7 and 10 sprint towards the near post and the goalkeeper respectively.
- Taking advantage of the screen on his opponent, 4 can freely move towards the penalty spot and shoot at goal.

Common mistakes: Timing of fakes and runs, either too late or too early.

Coaching notes: ────────────────────

_____

_____

_____

_____

_____

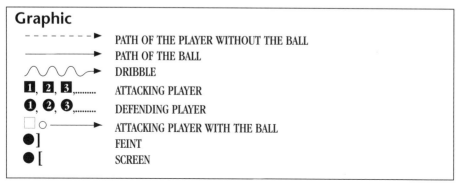

Graphic

┄┄┄┄┄►	PATH OF THE PLAYER WITHOUT THE BALL
─────►	PATH OF THE BALL
∿∿∿►	DRIBBLE
1, **2**, **3**,.........	ATTACKING PLAYER
❶, **❷**, **❸**,.........	DEFENDING PLAYER
□ ○ ────►	ATTACKING PLAYER WITH THE BALL
●]	FEINT
●[	SCREEN

Restarting the game at set plays:
Corner kick #18

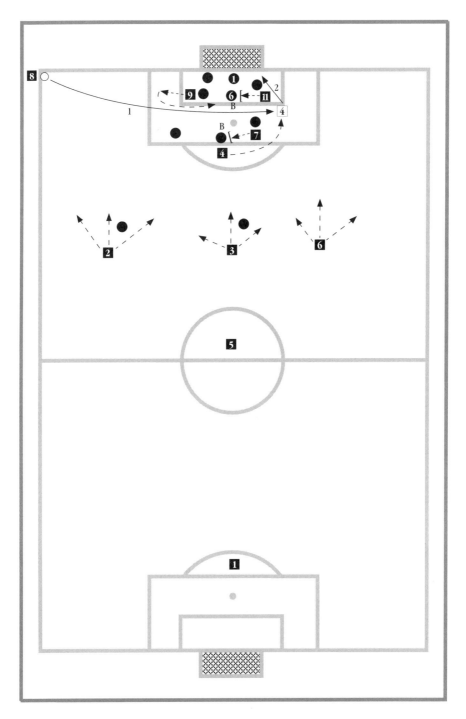

Technical-tactical purposes:
Clearing the space for a teammate at the far angle of the goal area, by means of an screen and a feint.
Conventional signal: 9 stands with his left hand on his head.

Equipment: Supply of balls, 11+ 11 players.

Area required: Half of soccer field.

Coaching methods: Deductive ➤ assigned tasks.

Description of the offensive situations:
- while 8 is about to kick the ball from the left corner of the field,
- 7 moves towards the opponent of 4 to perform the screen,
- and 11 prepares for a feint to distract the attention of his opponent ⑥.
- in this way, they clear the space for 4 to shoot at goal.

Common mistakes: Inaccurate corner kick, 11 fails to clear the area.

Coaching notes: _____

_____

_____

_____

_____

_____

_____

_____

_____

Graphic

- - - - - - ►	PATH OF THE PLAYER WITHOUT THE BALL
───────►	PATH OF THE BALL
∿∿∿►	DRIBBLE
1, **2**, **3**,.........	ATTACKING PLAYER
❶, ❷, ❸,.........	DEFENDING PLAYER
☐ ○ ───►	ATTACKING PLAYER WITH THE BALL
●]	FEINT
●[	SCREEN

Restarting the game at set plays:
Corner kick #19

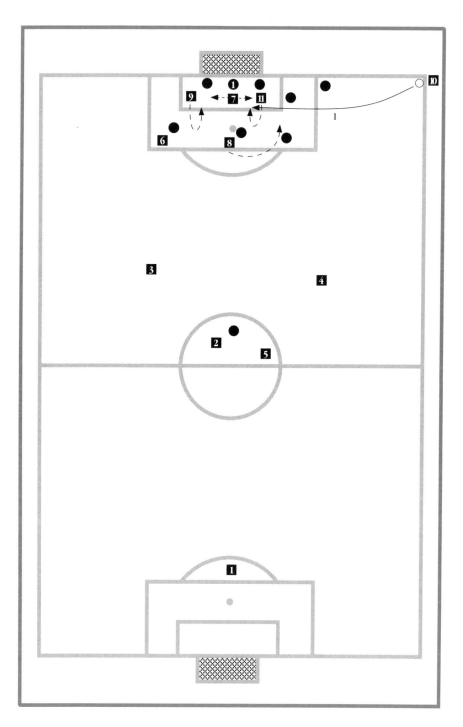

Technical-tactical purposes:
Clearing the goal area with rapid movements.
Conventional signal: 10 puts his right hand on his head.

Equipment: Supply of balls, 8 + 8.

Area required: Half of soccer field.

Coaching methods: Inductive ➤➤ guided discovery.

Description of the offensive situations:
- 7 performs a feint on the goalkeeper ①,
- meanwhile, 11 sprints out of the 6 yard box and then goes back rapidly;
- at the same time, 10 makes a firm pass into the path of the running 11, who has free space enough to shoot at goal.
- near the far post, 9 moves in the same way as 11, so that he is ready to meet the ball in case the goalkeeper ① kicks or fists it back.

Common mistakes: Feints made too early or too late.

Coaching notes: _____

_____

_____

_____

_____

_____

_____

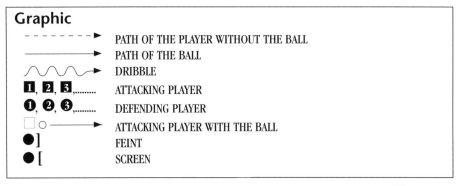

Graphic

- - - - - - ➤	PATH OF THE PLAYER WITHOUT THE BALL
——————➤	PATH OF THE BALL
∿∿∿∿➤	DRIBBLE
1, 2, 3,........	ATTACKING PLAYER
❶, ❷, ❸,........	DEFENDING PLAYER
☐○ ——➤	ATTACKING PLAYER WITH THE BALL
●]	FEINT
●[	SCREEN

Restarting the game at set plays:
Corner kick #20

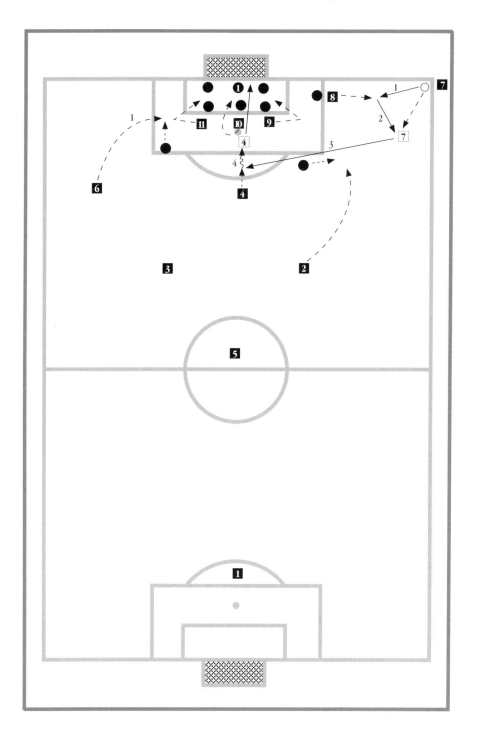

Technical-tactical purposes:
Clearing the space of the mid-goal area with suitable movements aimed at eluding the opponents' marking.

Equipment: Supply of balls, 11 + 11 players.

Area required: Half of soccer field.

Coaching methods: Inductive ➤➤ problem solving.

Description of the offensive situations:
- 7 kicks the ball to his teammate 8 , who passes it back to him.
- 9 , 10 , 11 move in such a way as to create space in the middle of the area;
- where 4 threads his way, sprinting from outside the 18 yard box.
- He receives the ball from his teammate 7 , dribbles, enters the goal area and shoots at goal.

Common mistakes: Inaccuracy of the final pass.

Coaching notes: _____

_____

_____

_____

_____

_____

_____

_____

_____

Graphic

– – – – – ▶	PATH OF THE PLAYER WITHOUT THE BALL
────▶	PATH OF THE BALL
∿∿∿▶	DRIBBLE
1, **2**, **3**,........	ATTACKING PLAYER
❶, ❷, ❸,........	DEFENDING PLAYER
□ ○ ────▶	ATTACKING PLAYER WITH THE BALL
●]	FEINT
●[	SCREEN

Restarting the game at set plays:
Corner kick #21

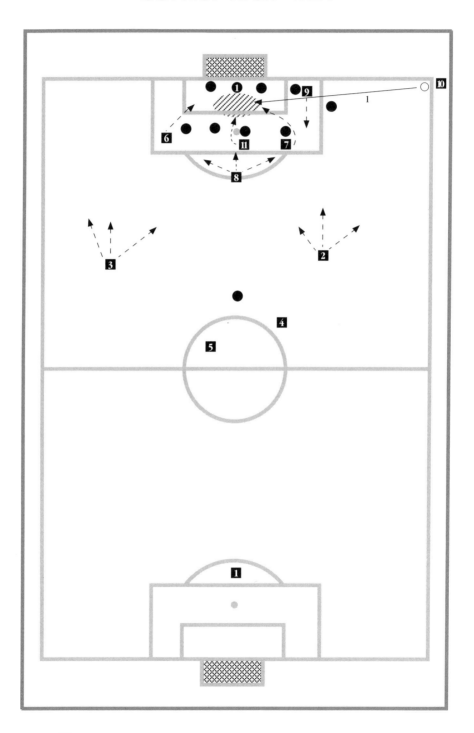

Technical-tactical purposes:
Flat and powerful corner kick aimed at the mid-goal area.

Equipment: Supply of balls, 11 + 11 players.

Area required: Half of soccer field.

Coaching methods: Inductive ➤ problem solving.

Description of the offensive situations:
* 10 kicks the ball with the left instep,
* after his central teammates 6, 11 and 7 have eluded the opponents' marking, they move towards the mid-goal area, where they are likely to exploit a favorable position to shoot at goal.

Common mistakes: Failure to communicate who will take the shot

Coaching notes: _____

_____

_____

_____

_____

_____

_____

_____

_____

_____

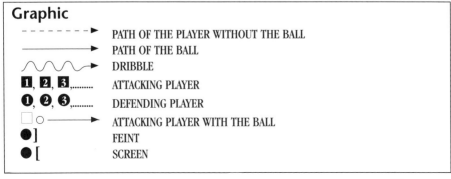

Graphic	
– – – – – –►	PATH OF THE PLAYER WITHOUT THE BALL
———►	PATH OF THE BALL
∿∿∿►	DRIBBLE
1, **2**, **3**,........	ATTACKING PLAYER
❶, ❷, ❸,........	DEFENDING PLAYER
▢○———►	ATTACKING PLAYER WITH THE BALL
●]	FEINT
●[	SCREEN

Restarting the game at set plays:
Corner kick #22

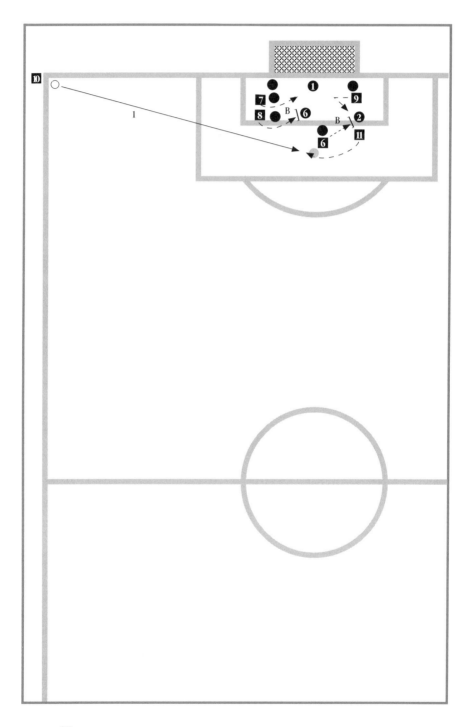

Technical-tactical purposes:
Creating space near the penalty spot, by performing two screens.

Equipment: Supply of balls, 6 + 8 players.

Area required: Half of soccer field.

Coaching methods: Deductive ➻ assigned tasks.

Description of the offensive situations:
- 10 kicks the ball with the left instep towards the penalty spot,
- in the meantime, 8 and 6 perform screens on their opponents,
- in this way, 11 is free to move towards the ball and can easily shoot at goal.

Common mistakes: Inaccurate corner kick.

Coaching notes: _____

_____

_____

_____

_____

_____

_____

_____

_____

_____

_____

Graphic

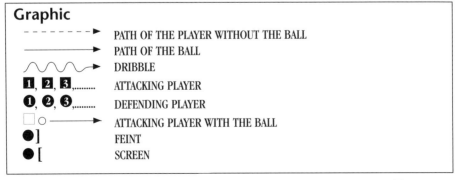

- - - ►	PATH OF THE PLAYER WITHOUT THE BALL
——►	PATH OF THE BALL
∿∿∿►	DRIBBLE
1, 2, 3,........	ATTACKING PLAYER
❶, ❷, ❸,........	DEFENDING PLAYER
☐ ○——►	ATTACKING PLAYER WITH THE BALL
●]	FEINT
●[	SCREEN

Restarting the game at set plays:
Free kick #1

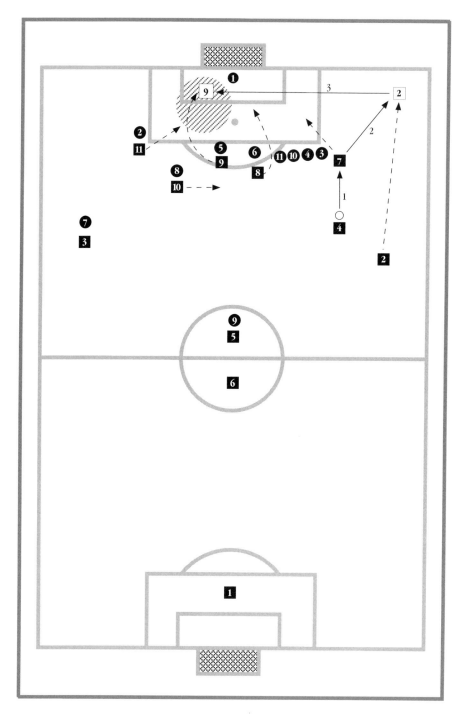

Technical-tactical purposes:
Indirect free kick from the right; cross parallel to the line of the goal area.
Penetration of the right back from behind.

Equipment: Supply of balls, 11 + 11 players.

Area required: Half of soccer field.

Coaching methods: Deductive ➤ assigned tasks.

Description of the offensive situations:
- 4 kicks the ball to his teammate 7 ,
- who plays it with a diagonal pass on the line of the run of 2 , sprinting from behind,
- 2 kicks the ball with the right instep parallel to the horizontal line of the 6 yard box,
- in the meantime, 9 breaks through the defensive line and shoots at goal with a volley.

Common mistakes: Cross made too close to the goalkeeper.
9 makes his run too early.

Coaching notes: ———————————————————————

————————————————————————————————————

————————————————————————————————————

————————————————————————————————————

————————————————————————————————————

————————————————————————————————————

Graphic

- - - - - - - ➤	PATH OF THE PLAYER WITHOUT THE BALL
———————➤	PATH OF THE BALL
∿∿∿∿➤	DRIBBLE
1, **2**, **3**,.........	ATTACKING PLAYER
❶, **❷**, **❸**,.........	DEFENDING PLAYER
☐ ○ ———➤	ATTACKING PLAYER WITH THE BALL
●]	FEINT
● [	SCREEN

Restarting the game at set plays:
Free kick #2

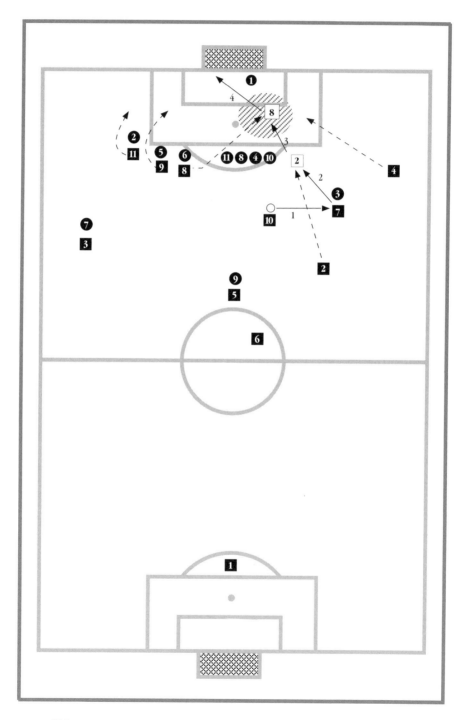

Technical-tactical purposes:
Central free kick with ball combinations between three players.

Equipment: Supply of balls, 11 + 11 players.

Area required: Half of soccer field.

Coaching methods: Deductive ➥ assigned tasks.

Description of the offensive situations:
- 10 passes the ball to his teammate 7 , who controls it and then plays it towards the running 2 .
- 2 makes an accurate zone-pass inviting 8 to break through the defensive line to take part in the offensive combination,
- 8 shoots at goal with the right instep.

Common mistakes: Final pass too firm, must be played into space and weighted correctly.

Coaching notes: _____

_____

_____

_____

_____

_____

_____

_____

_____

_____

Graphic

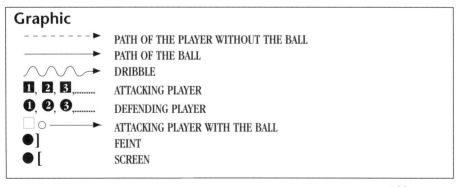

- – – – – ➤ PATH OF THE PLAYER WITHOUT THE BALL
- ——————➤ PATH OF THE BALL
- ∿∿∿➤ DRIBBLE
- **1**, **2**, **3**,......... ATTACKING PLAYER
- **❶**, **❷**, **❸**,......... DEFENDING PLAYER
- ☐ ○ ——➤ ATTACKING PLAYER WITH THE BALL
- ●] FEINT
- ●[SCREEN

Restarting the game at set plays:
Free kick #3

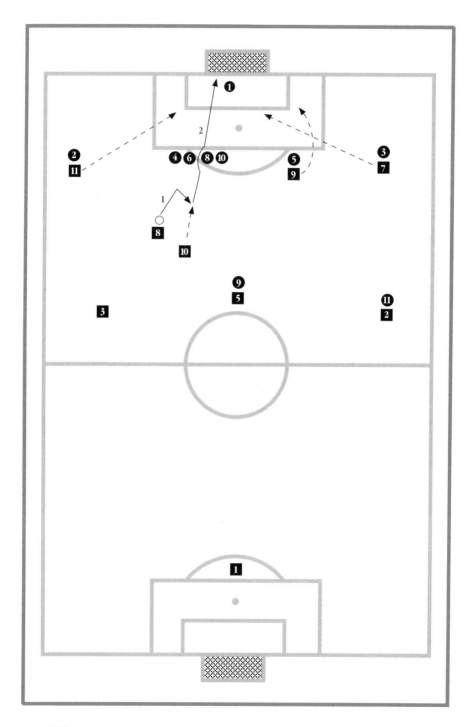

Technical-tactical purposes:
Free kick taken by lobbing the ball.
Volley shot with the left instep over the wall.

Equipment: Supply of balls, 11 + 11 players.

Area required: Half of soccer field.

Coaching methods: Deductive ➡ guided discovery.

Description of the offensive situations:
- 8 pretends to give a pass to his teammate 9 , but he then lobs the ball, vertically, for 10 .
- 10 volleys the ball with the left instep, aiming it at the near post

Common mistakes: Inaccuracy and/or lack of timing in the lob pass.

Coaching notes: _____

_____

_____

_____

_____

_____

_____

_____

_____

_____

_____

Graphic

– – – – – ►	PATH OF THE PLAYER WITHOUT THE BALL
──────►	PATH OF THE BALL
∿∿∿►	DRIBBLE
1, **2**, **3**,.........	ATTACKING PLAYER
❶, ❷, ❸,.........	DEFENDING PLAYER
☐○────►	ATTACKING PLAYER WITH THE BALL
●]	FEINT
●[	SCREEN

Restarting the game at set plays:
Free kick #4

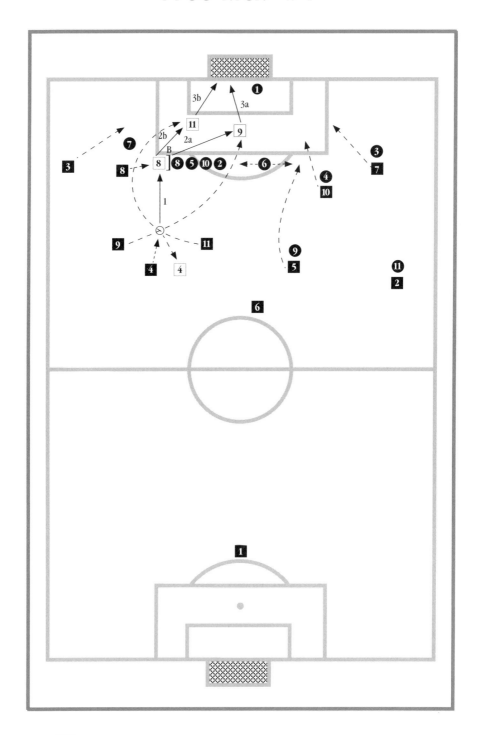

Technical-tactical purposes:
Indirect free kick from the left
Screen on the opponent ⑧ standing in the defensive wall.

Equipment: Supply of balls, 11 + 11 players.

Area required: Half of soccer field.

Coaching methods: Deductive ➳ assigned tasks.

Description of the offensive situations:
- players ⑪ and ⑨ cross each other, running over the ball.
- ④ plays the ball to ⑧ just at the moment when he is arriving near the wall to perform the screen on his opponent ⑧.
- According to the space and the time available, ⑧ can play the ball to ⑪ or to ⑨, who are in favorable positions to shoot at goal.

Common mistakes:
⑧ is not quick enough in his decision and the pass is too late (⑨ and ⑪ are offside).

Coaching notes: ───────────────────────────

_____

_____

_____

_____

_____

_____

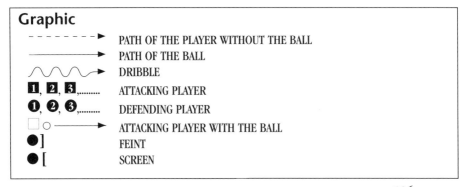

Graphic

- - - - - ➤	PATH OF THE PLAYER WITHOUT THE BALL
─────➤	PATH OF THE BALL
∿∿∿➤	DRIBBLE
1, **2**, **3**,.........	ATTACKING PLAYER
❶, ❷, ❸,.........	DEFENDING PLAYER
☐ ○ ─────➤	ATTACKING PLAYER WITH THE BALL
●]	FEINT
●[	SCREEN

Restarting the game at set plays:
Free kick #5

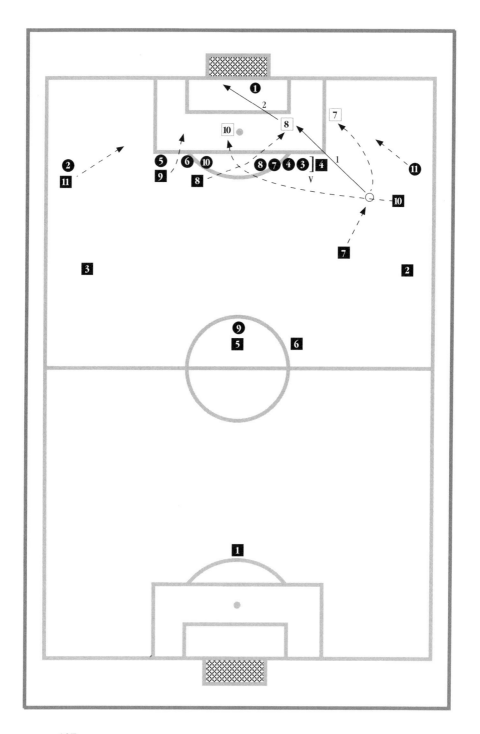

Technical-tactical purposes:
Free kick from the right.
Performing the screen and eluding the opponents' marking.

Equipment: Supply of balls, 11 + 11 players.

Area required: Half of soccer field.

Coaching methods: Deductive ➤ assigned tasks.

Description of the offensive situations:
- 10 runs towards the ball and pretends to kick, but he then runs on towards the penalty spot.
- 7 follows him and kicks the ball towards the right angle of the opposing goal area (screen performed by 4);
- after a cross-over run, 8 converges on the ball and shoots at goal with the right instep.
- 7 , 9 , 10 , 11 enter the penalty box so that they are ready to intervene in case the goalkeeper clears the ball.

Common mistakes: Timing of the runs either too late or too early

Coaching notes: _____

_____

_____

_____

_____

_____

_____

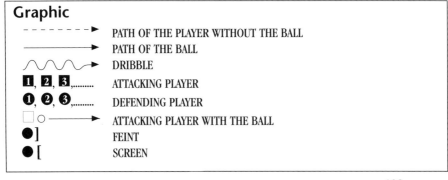

Graphic
– – – – – – ➤	PATH OF THE PLAYER WITHOUT THE BALL
———➤	PATH OF THE BALL
∿∿∿➤	DRIBBLE
1, 2, 3,.........	ATTACKING PLAYER
❶, ❷, ❸,.........	DEFENDING PLAYER
☐ ○ ———➤	ATTACKING PLAYER WITH THE BALL
●]	FEINT
●[	SCREEN

Restarting the game at set plays:
Free kick #6

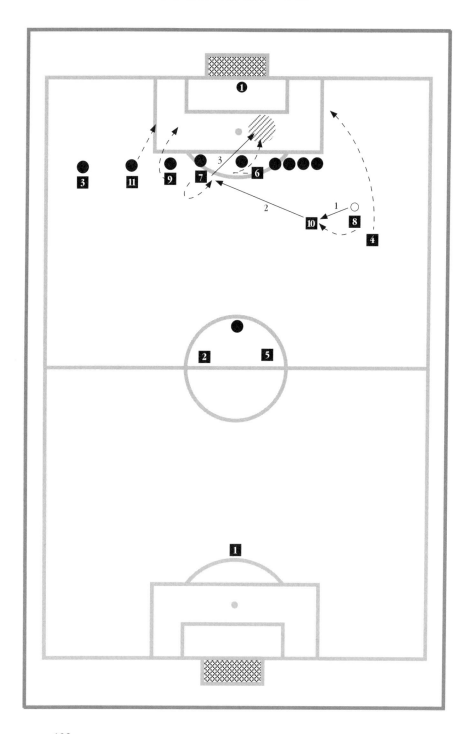

Technical-tactical purposes:
Creating space in front of the defensive wall.
Feinting and eluding the opponents' marking.

Equipment: Supply of balls, 11 + 11 players

Area required: Half of soccer field

Coaching methods: Deductive ➡ prescriptive

Description of the offensive situations:
- 8 pretends to shoot at goal, but he plays the ball to 10.
- 10 stops the ball under the sole of his foot and makes a pass to 7;
- after feinting to move off the arc of the circle, 7 runs back and gives an accurate zone-pass for the running 6, who shoots at goal.
- 4, 9, 10 promptly enter the penalty area to exploit a possible clearance by the goalkeeper.

Common mistakes: Inaccurate final pass into space.

Coaching notes: _____

_____

_____

_____

_____

_____

_____

Graphic

- - - - - ►	PATH OF THE PLAYER WITHOUT THE BALL
───►	PATH OF THE BALL
∿∿∿►	DRIBBLE
1, **2**, **3**,.........	ATTACKING PLAYER
❶, **❷**, **❸**,.........	DEFENDING PLAYER
☐ ○───►	ATTACKING PLAYER WITH THE BALL
●]	FEINT
●[	SCREEN

Restarting the game at set plays:
Free kick #7

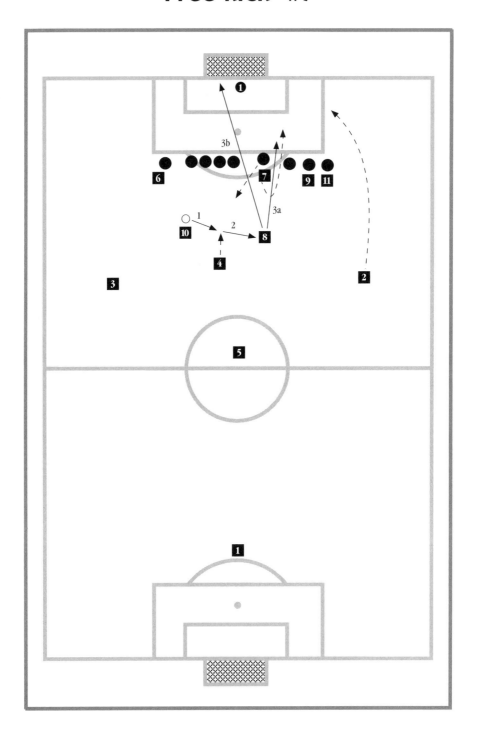

Technical-tactical purposes:
Creating central space for a shot at goal taken from outside the penalty area or for the upward penetration of a central forward.

Equipment: Supply of balls, 11 + 11 players.

Area required: Half of soccer field.

Coaching methods: Deductive ➺ assigned tasks.

Description of the offensive situations:
- $\boxed{10}$ passes the ball to his teammate $\boxed{4}$, who stops it under the sole of his shoe and immediately plays it to $\boxed{8}$, as he is challenged by an opponent;
- $\boxed{8}$ has two possibilities:
    1. shooting directly at goal;
    2. making a through pass for $\boxed{7}$ who has got free from his opponent's marking in a central position.

Common mistakes: $\boxed{8}$ delays in his decision making, allowing defense to converge.

Coaching notes: _____

_____

_____

_____

_____

_____

_____

_____

Graphic

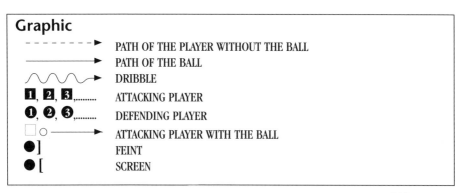

- - - - - - ➤   PATH OF THE PLAYER WITHOUT THE BALL
————➤   PATH OF THE BALL
∿∿∿➤   DRIBBLE
1, **2**, **3**,.........   ATTACKING PLAYER
❶, **❷**, **❸**,.........   DEFENDING PLAYER
▢○————➤   ATTACKING PLAYER WITH THE BALL
●]   FEINT
●[SCREEN

Restarting the game at set plays:
Free kick #8

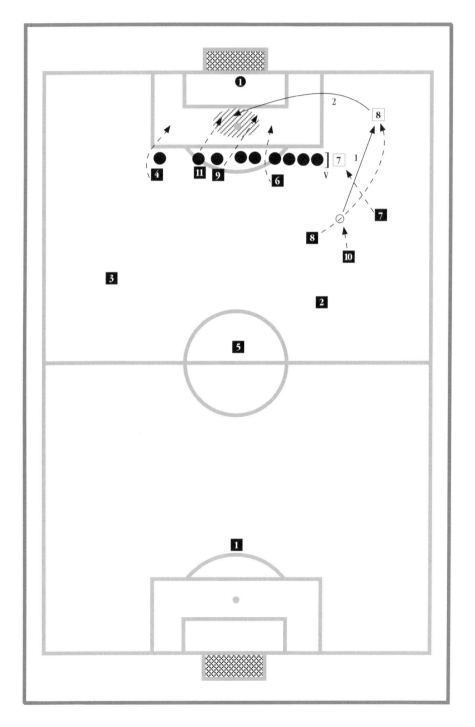

Technical-tactical purposes:
Free kick with an overlapping run on the right side.

Equipment: Supply of balls, 11 + 11 players.

Area required: Half of soccer field.

Coaching methods: Deductive ➻ assigned tasks.

Description of the offensive situations:

- 8 begins to run, passes over the ball and keeps on running in a semi-circle, waiting for a through pass made by 10.
- Meanwhile, 7 runs towards the center and performs a feint movement on the first opponent standing at the right end of the defensive wall.
- The players 4, 11, 9 and 6 sprint into the penalty area, waiting for the cross of 8.

Common mistakes: Initial pass given too late, disrupting timing of the play.

Coaching notes:

Graphic

- - - - - - - -►	PATH OF THE PLAYER WITHOUT THE BALL
————►	PATH OF THE BALL
∿∿∿∿►	DRIBBLE
1, 2, 3,.........	ATTACKING PLAYER
❶, ❷, ❸,.........	DEFENDING PLAYER
□ ○ ————►	ATTACKING PLAYER WITH THE BALL
●]	FEINT
●[	SCREEN

Restarting the game at set plays:
Free kick #9

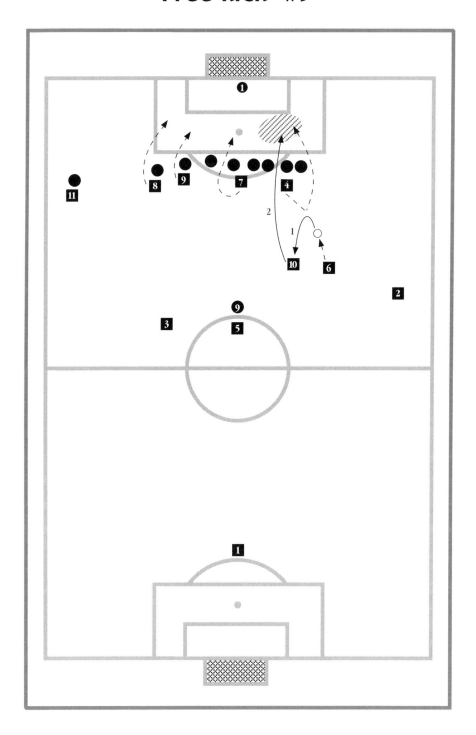

Technical-tactical purposes:
Creating space behind the defensive wall.

Equipment: Supply of balls, 11 + 11 players.

Area required: Half of soccer field.

Coaching methods: Deductive ➤➤ assigned tasks.

Description of the offensive situations:
- [6] lofts the ball for his teammate [10], who kicks it towards the penalty area, just beyond the wall.
- [4] first feints to run to meet the ball and then sprints beyond the defensive wall in order to receive the lob made by [10].
- the players [8], [9], [7] perform some feint movements and then run into the penalty box, following the directions previously agreed upon.

Common mistakes: Final lob pass too short or too long.

Coaching notes: —————————————————————

——————————————————————————————————

——————————————————————————————————

——————————————————————————————————

——————————————————————————————————

——————————————————————————————————

——————————————————————————————————

——————————————————————————————————

——————————————————————————————————

Graphic

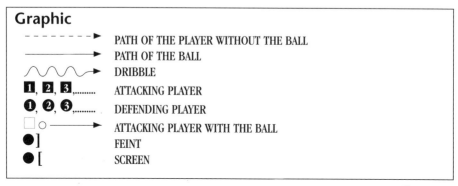

- - - - - - - ▶   PATH OF THE PLAYER WITHOUT THE BALL
————————▶   PATH OF THE BALL
∿∿∿∿▶   DRIBBLE
1, **2**, **3**,..........   ATTACKING PLAYER
❶, **❷**, **❸**,..........   DEFENDING PLAYER
☐ ○ ————▶   ATTACKING PLAYER WITH THE BALL
●]   FEINT
●[SCREEN

Restarting the game at set plays:
Free kick #10

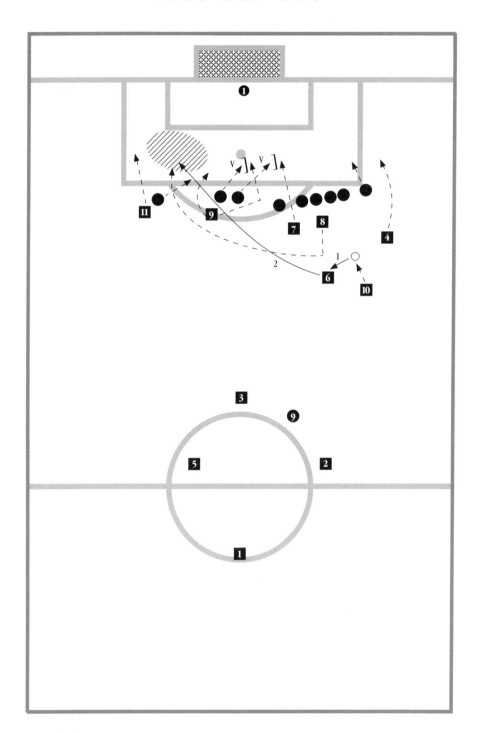

Technical-tactical purposes:
Diverting movements useful to clear the left area of the penalty box.

Equipment: Supply of balls, 11 + 11 players.

Area required: Half of soccer field.

Coaching methods: Deductive ➥ prescriptive.

Description of the offensive situations:
- 10 plays the ball to his teammate 6 , who stops it under the sole of his shoe.
- with the left instep 10 kicks the ball towards the area marked in the diagram, for the running 8 .
- The players 9 and 7 can perform feint movements on their two central opponents.
- 4 sprints on the right side of the penalty area to meet a possible pass made by 8 or a clearance by the goalkeeper.

Common mistakes: 8 makes his run too wide or too late.

Coaching notes: _____

_____

_____

_____

_____

_____

_____

_____

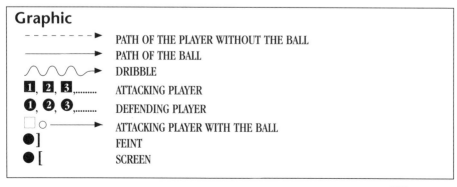

Graphic

‑ ‑ ‑ ‑ ‑ ‑►	PATH OF THE PLAYER WITHOUT THE BALL
───────►	PATH OF THE BALL
∿∿∿►	DRIBBLE
1, **2**, **3**,………	ATTACKING PLAYER
❶, ❷, ❸,………	DEFENDING PLAYER
□ ○ ───►	ATTACKING PLAYER WITH THE BALL
●]	FEINT
●[	SCREEN

Restarting the game at set plays:
Free kick #11

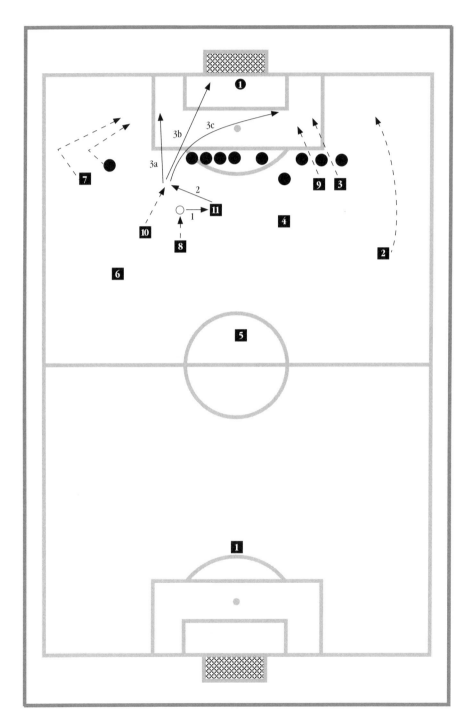

Technical-tactical purposes:
Creating different solutions for the last pass.

Equipment: Supply of balls, 11 + 11 players.

Area required: Half of soccer field.

Coaching methods: Deductive ➳ assigned tasks.

Description of the offensive situations:
- 8 restarts the game with a free kick; he passes the ball to his teammate 11 .
- 11 feints to stop to shoot at goal, but then he gives a diagonal pass, leftward, on the line of the run of 10 .
- 10 has three alternative solutions:
  1. making the last pass for the penetrations of 9 and 3 on the right side;
  2. giving a through pass for the overlapping run of 7 ;
  3. directly shooting at goal from a position outside the penalty area.

Common mistakes: 10 delays in his decision making, allowing the defense to converge.

Coaching notes: _____

_____

_____

_____

_____

_____

_____

Graphic
- - - - - - ▶ PATH OF THE PLAYER WITHOUT THE BALL
———▶ PATH OF THE BALL
〜〜〜▶ DRIBBLE
1, **2**, **3**,.......... ATTACKING PLAYER
❶, ❷, ❸,.......... DEFENDING PLAYER
□ ○———▶ ATTACKING PLAYER WITH THE BALL
●] FEINT
●[SCREEN

Restarting the game at set plays:
Free kick #12

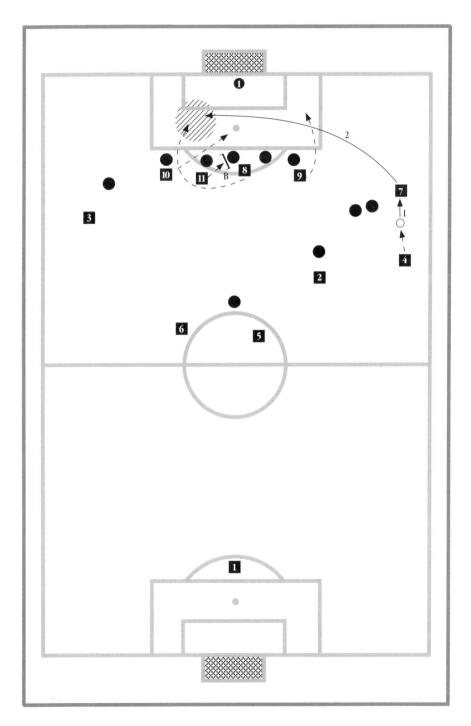

Technical-tactical purposes:
Clearing space within the penalty area by means of a screen in the central lane.

Equipment: Supply of balls, 11 + 11 players.

Area required: Half of soccer field.

Coaching methods: Deductive ➤➤ assigned tasks.

Description of the offensive situations:
- ☐4 plays the ball to his teammate ☐7 on the right flank of the field;
- ☐7 makes a diagonal pass towards the far angle of the goal area (the left one).
- As soon as ☐4 begins to run, ☐11 sprints centrally to obstruct the defender of ☐8 , so as to help his teammate elude his opponent's marking and break through the 18 yard box.
- ☐10 and ☐9 follow the play eluding the marking of their respective opponents.

Common mistakes: ☐8 makes his run either to early or too late.

Coaching notes: _____

_____

_____

_____

_____

_____

_____

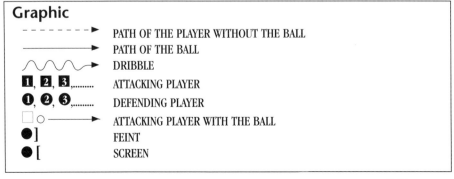

Graphic
- - - - - - - ▶	PATH OF THE PLAYER WITHOUT THE BALL
─────▶	PATH OF THE BALL
∿∿∿▶	DRIBBLE
1, **2**, **3**,........	ATTACKING PLAYER
❶, **❷**, **❸**,........	DEFENDING PLAYER
☐ ○ ────▶	ATTACKING PLAYER WITH THE BALL
●]	FEINT
●[	SCREEN

Restarting the game at set plays:
Free kick #13

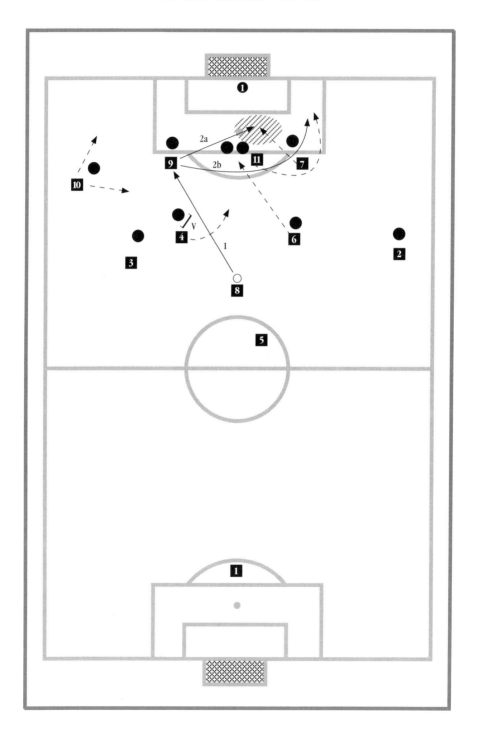

Technical-tactical purposes:
Creating space at a central free kick.

Equipment: Supply of balls, 11 + 11 players.

Area required: Half of soccer field.

Coaching methods: Deductive ➔ prescriptive.

Description of the offensive situations:
- [8] makes a pass in the direction of [4];
- [4] feints and lets the ball roll on to [9], who directly plays it on the line of the run of his teammate [7] or lofts the ball for [11], who is unexpectedly breaking through the penalty area.

Common mistakes: [9] is indecisive, affecting accuracy of the final pass.

Coaching notes: _____

_____

_____

_____

_____

_____

_____

_____

_____

_____

Graphic

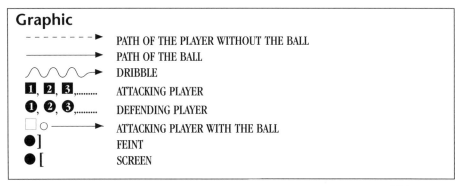

- - - - - ➤	PATH OF THE PLAYER WITHOUT THE BALL
———➤	PATH OF THE BALL
∿∿∿➤	DRIBBLE
∎, ▨, ▣,..........	ATTACKING PLAYER
❶, ❷, ❸,..........	DEFENDING PLAYER
☐ ○ ———➤	ATTACKING PLAYER WITH THE BALL
●]	FEINT
●[	SCREEN

Restarting the game at set plays:
Free kick #14

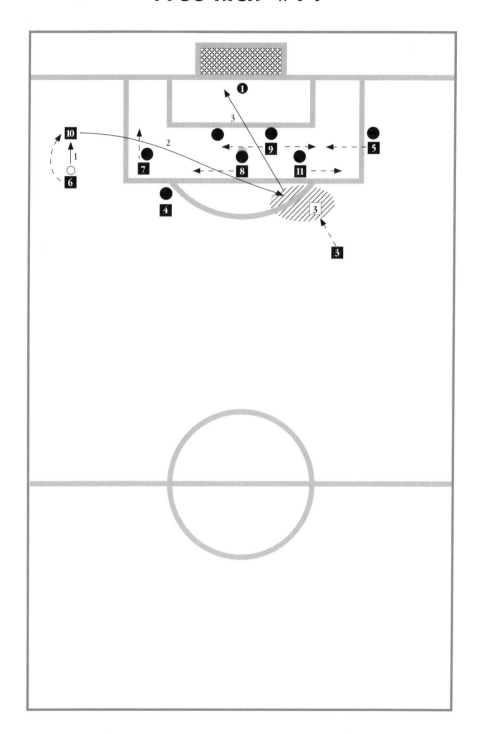

Technical-tactical purposes:
Creating space within the penalty area for a shot from outside.

Equipment: Supply of balls, 11 + 11 players.

Area required: Half of the field.

Coaching methods: Deductive ➟ assigned tasks.

Description of the offensive situations:
- [6] gives a short pass to [10];
- [10] stops the ball for [6] who is overlapping him; [6] kicks with the left instep.
- the ball makes a 'soft' arc and lands just outside the 18 yard box, in the central area, where [3] is arriving to volley at goal.
- the players [8] and [11] run sideways thus creating further space and clearing the area for their teammate [3] ;
- [9] and [5] act as a shield just in front of the goalkeeper.

Common mistakes: Runs to create space ([8] and [11]) made too early, allowing defense to recover.

Coaching notes: _____

_____

_____

_____

_____

_____

_____

Graphic

- - - - - - - ►   PATH OF THE PLAYER WITHOUT THE BALL
——————►   PATH OF THE BALL
〜〜〜〜►   DRIBBLE
1, **2**, **3**,.........   ATTACKING PLAYER
❶, **❷**, **❸**,.........   DEFENDING PLAYER
□ ○ ——————►   ATTACKING PLAYER WITH THE BALL
●]   FEINT
●[SCREEN

Restarting the game at set plays:
Free kick #15

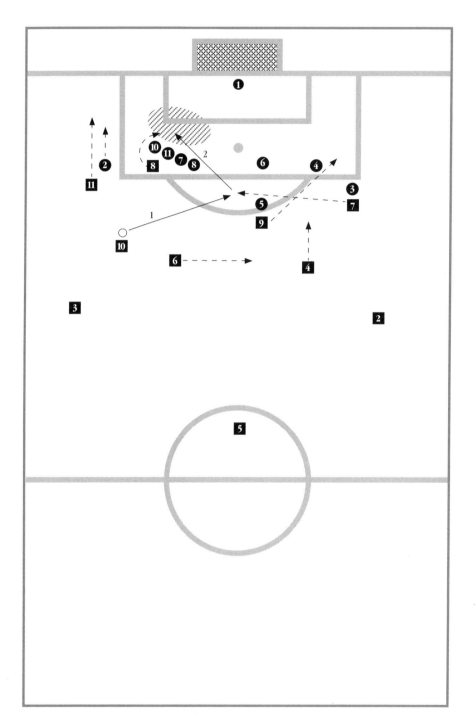

Technical-tactical purposes:
Shifting positions and faking.

Equipment: Supply of balls, 11 + 11 players.

Area required: Half of soccer field.

Coaching methods: Deductive ➸ assigned tasks.

Description of the offensive situations:
- 10 feints a pass to 6, but he plays the ball to his teammate 7 who is running towards the center.
- 7 directly kicks the ball towards the left angle of the opposing goal area, where 8 is running at the right moment to shoot at goal.

Common mistakes: 8 makes his run either too early or too late.

Coaching notes: ______________________________

____

____

____

____

____

____

____

____

____

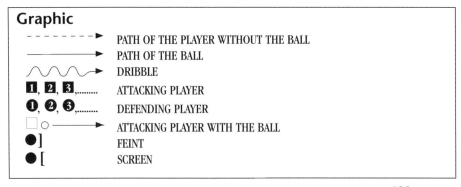

Graphic

- - - - - - - -►	PATH OF THE PLAYER WITHOUT THE BALL
————————►	PATH OF THE BALL
∿∿∿∿►	DRIBBLE
■1, ■2, ■3,.........	ATTACKING PLAYER
❶, ❷, ❸,.........	DEFENDING PLAYER
□ ○ ————►	ATTACKING PLAYER WITH THE BALL
●]	FEINT
●[	SCREEN

Restarting the game at set plays:
Penalty kick #1

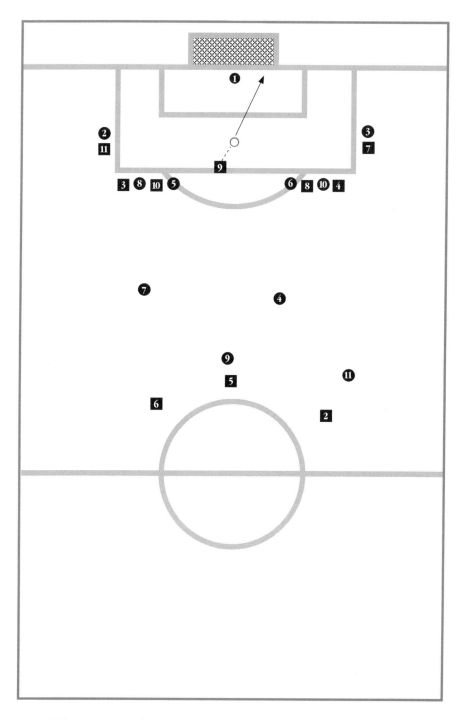

Technical-tactical purposes:
Scoring directly at the penalty kick; kicking the ball with the right instep.

Equipment: Supply of balls, 1 + goalkeeper.

Area required: Penalty area.

Coaching methods: Inductive ➠ guided discovery.

Description of the offensive and defensive situations:
- 9 is the penalty kicker; while moving towards the penalty spot to place the ball, he tries to keep the greatest concentration.
- He takes a short run starting from the left and describing an arc (about 3 yards); he feints left and then kicks the ball with the right instep.
- The ball is kicked into the goal at the left of the goalkeeper (mid-height trajectory).
- all the attacking players standing outside the penalty area are ready to intervene in case the ball is cleared by the goalkeeper or by one of the posts.
- the defenders ⑤ and ⑥ should previously move towards the two opposing ends of the arc of the circle. In this way, together with their defending teammates, they are ready to intervene to create the opportunity for a possible counterattack.

Common mistakes: Lack of concentration.

Coaching notes: _____

_____

_____

_____

Graphic

- - - - - ➤	PATH OF THE PLAYER WITHOUT THE BALL
────➤	PATH OF THE BALL
∿∿∿➤	DRIBBLE
1, **2**, **3**,........	ATTACKING PLAYER
❶, ❷, ❸,........	DEFENDING PLAYER
☐○────➤	ATTACKING PLAYER WITH THE BALL
●]	FEINT
●[	SCREEN

Restarting the game at set plays:
Penalty kick #2

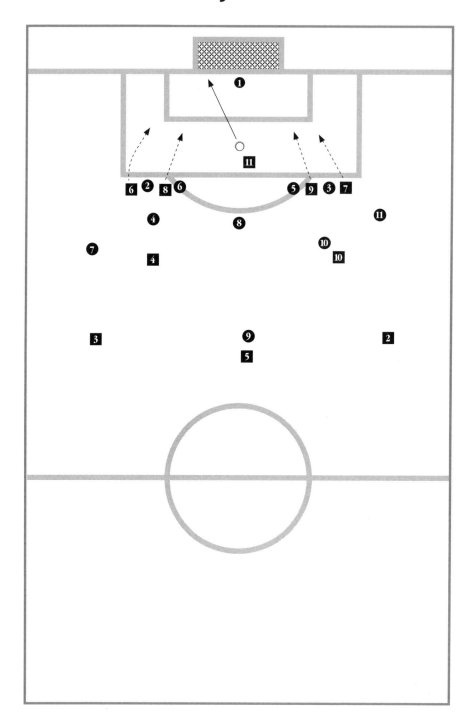

Technical-tactical purposes:
Penalty kick; shoot with the left instep.

Equipment: Supply of balls, 1 + goalkeeper.

Area required: Penalty area.

Coaching methods: Deductive ➡ prescriptive.

Description of the offensive situations:
- [11] is the penalty kicker.
- He takes a short run describing a curve-like path and kicks the ball with the left instep.
- The ball enters the goal very close to the post, grazing the ground.

Common mistakes: Lack of concentration.

Coaching notes: _____

_____

_____

_____

_____

_____

_____

_____

_____

_____

Graphic

- - - - - - ➤	PATH OF THE PLAYER WITHOUT THE BALL
⸻➤	PATH OF THE BALL
∿∿∿➤	DRIBBLE
1, **2**, **3**,.........	ATTACKING PLAYER
❶, **❷**, **❸**,.........	DEFENDING PLAYER
☐ ○ ⸻➤	ATTACKING PLAYER WITH THE BALL
●]	FEINT
●[	SCREEN

Restarting the game at set plays:
Penalty kick #3

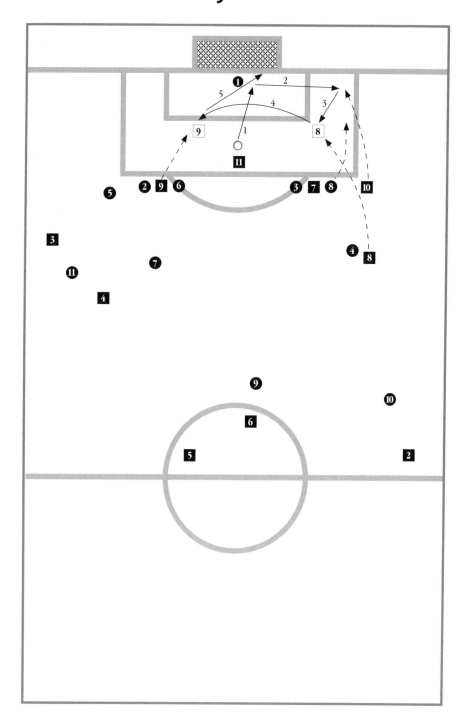

Technical-tactical purposes:
Penalty kick; shoot with the right instep (volleying the ball from a stationary position).

Equipment: Supply of balls, 11 + 11 players.

Area required: Half of the field.

Coaching methods: Deductive ➤➤ mixed.

Description of the offensive situations:
- when the referee blows his whistle, the attacking player $\boxed{11}$ starts from a central position, runs towards the ball on the penalty spot and shoots at goal with the instep.
- the goalkeeper intercepts the ball and fists it away towards the left sideline.
- the forward $\boxed{10}$ immediately sprints to meet the ball, followed by the defender Ⓐ.
- $\boxed{10}$ directly passes the ball to his teammate $\boxed{8}$, who kicks it back towards the free area near the forward $\boxed{9}$ as soon as possible,
- $\boxed{9}$ anticipates all the other players and volleys at goal with the right instep.

Common mistakes: Slow reaction to the saved penalty.

Coaching notes: _____

_____

_____

_____

_____

_____

Graphic

– – – – – ▶	PATH OF THE PLAYER WITHOUT THE BALL
——————▶	PATH OF THE BALL
∿∿∿∿▶	DRIBBLE
1, **2**, **3**,........	ATTACKING PLAYER
❶, ❷, ❸,........	DEFENDING PLAYER
☐○——▶	ATTACKING PLAYER WITH THE BALL
●]	FEINT
●[	SCREEN

Restarting the game at set plays:
Penalty kick #4

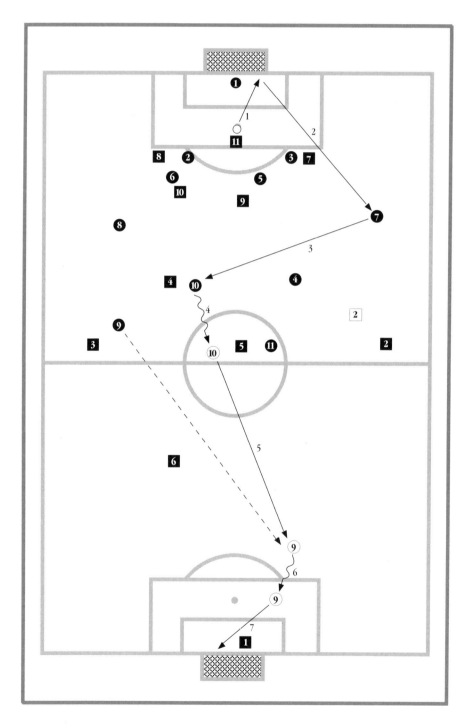

Technical-tactical purposes:
Penalty kick against; counter-attack and shot at goal.

Equipment: Supply of balls, 11 + 11 players.

Area required: Regulation soccer field.

Coaching methods: Deductive ➤➤ assigned tasks.

Description of the offensive situations:
- [11] kicks the penalty kick;
- the goalkeeper ① saves the shot and immediately plays the ball to his teammate ⑦;
- ⑦ gives a diagonal pass to ⑩ who, after dribbling the ball for some yards, makes a zone pass for his teammate ⑨;
- ⑨ gains possession of the ball, dribbles as far as the edge of the opposing penalty box and shoots at goal, striking the ball with the left instep.

Common mistakes: Failure of the players to react to the transition from defense to attack, and attack to defense.

Coaching notes: _____

_____

_____

_____

_____

_____

_____

_____

Graphic

`- - - - - - ▶`	PATH OF THE PLAYER WITHOUT THE BALL
`——————▶`	PATH OF THE BALL
`∿∿∿▶`	DRIBBLE
1, **2**, **3**,........	ATTACKING PLAYER
❶, ❷, ❸,........	DEFENDING PLAYER
☐ ○ ——▶	ATTACKING PLAYER WITH THE BALL
●]	FEINT
●[	SCREEN

Restarting the game at set plays:
Penalty kick #5

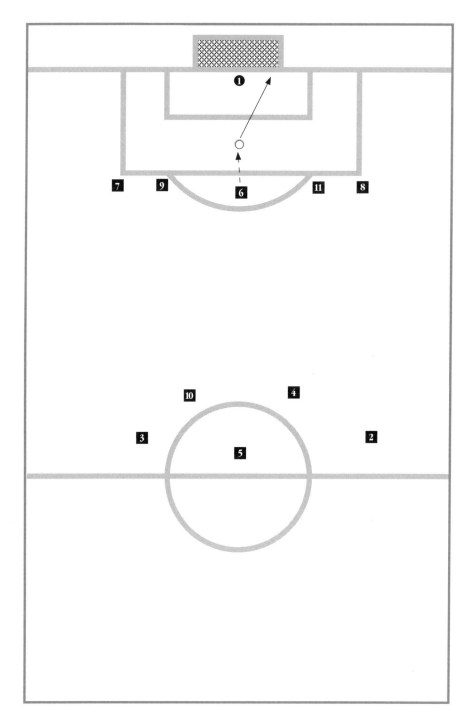

Technical-tactical purposes:
Penalty kick. . .when the team knows the abilities of the opponent goalkeeper.

Equipment: Supply of balls, 1 + goalkeeper.

Area required: Half of soccer field.

Coaching methods: Inductive ➡ guided discovery.

Description of the offensive situations:
*   6 , who is about to shoot the penalty kick, tries to concentrate, breathing deeply and slowly;
*   he places the ball on the penalty spot properly.
*   he takes a short run, the rhythm of his pace is now automatic and marked by constant training. Looking at the goalkeeper, he strikes a ground shot to the left of his opponent.
*   7 , 9 , 11 , 8 are concentrated and ready to intervene in case the goalkeeper clears the ball.
*   3 , 10 , 5 , 4 , 2 are ready to move in case the opponent wins possession of the ball and begins a counter-attack.

Common mistakes: Player taking the kick 'thinks' too much and loses his focus.

Coaching notes: _____

_____

_____

_____

_____

_____

Graphic

– – – – – – ▶	PATH OF THE PLAYER WITHOUT THE BALL
——————▶	PATH OF THE BALL
∿∿∿▶	DRIBBLE
1, **2**, **3**,........	ATTACKING PLAYER
❶, **❷**, **❸**,........	DEFENDING PLAYER
☐ ○ ——▶	ATTACKING PLAYER WITH THE BALL
●]	FEINT
● [	SCREEN

Restarting the game at set plays:
Throw-in #1

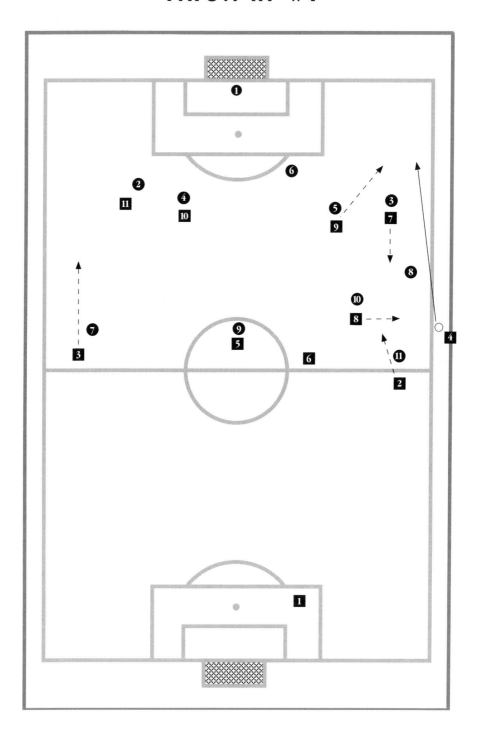

Technical-tactical purposes:
Throw-in just beyond the halfway line, on the right side.

Equipment: Supply of balls, 11 + 11 players.

Area required: Regulation soccer field.

Coaching methods: Deductive ➻ assigned tasks.

Description of the offensive situations:
- while 4 is about to throw in,
- 7 and 8 , respectively marked by ③ and ⑩, move near the point of the throw-in.
- 4 throws the ball on the line of the run of his teammate 9 , who controls it and dribbles to gain space forward.

Common mistakes: Runs not made simultaneously, allowing the defense to recover.

Coaching notes: _____

_____

_____

_____

_____

_____

_____

_____

_____

Graphic

- - - - ➤	PATH OF THE PLAYER WITHOUT THE BALL
——➤	PATH OF THE BALL
∿∿∿➤	DRIBBLE
1, **2**, **3**,.........	ATTACKING PLAYER
❶, ❷, ❸,.........	DEFENDING PLAYER
☐ ○ ——➤	ATTACKING PLAYER WITH THE BALL
●]	FEINT
●[	SCREEN

Restarting the game at set plays:
Throw-in #2

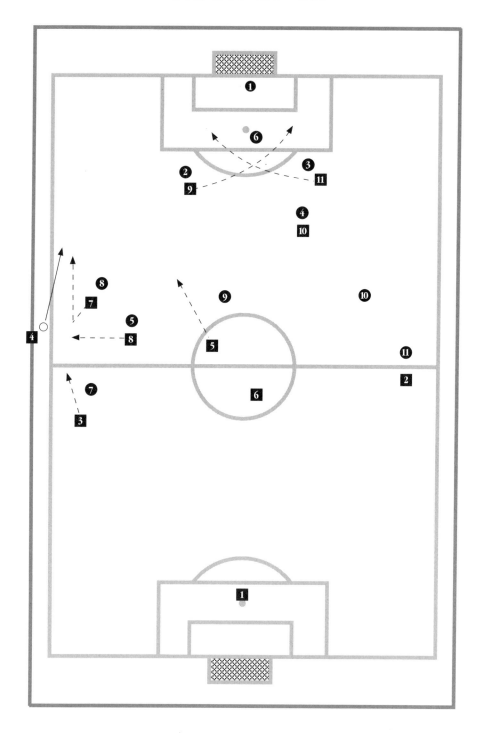

Technical-tactical purposes:
Throw-in just beyond the halfway line, on the left side.

Equipment: Supply of balls, 11 + 11 players.

Area required: Regulation soccer field.

Coaching methods: Deductive ➡ assigned tasks.

Description of the offensive situations:
- [4] throws in.
- [7] feints a movement towards his teammate, but then rapidly sprints forward to receive the ball.
- in the meantime, [9] and [11] perform a cross-over play in the central area,
- they try to concentrate so that they are both ready to shoot at goal directly on a pass from the left flank of the field.

Common mistakes: [7] fails to 'sell' his feint, allowing his marker to contain him.

Coaching notes: _____

_____

_____

_____

_____

_____

_____

_____

Graphic
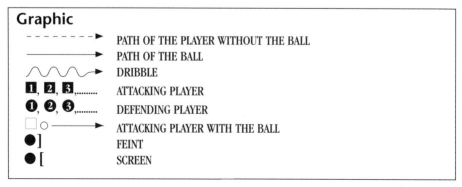

Restarting the game at set plays:
Throw-in #3

Technical-tactical purposes:
Throw-in in the offensive third of the field, on the right side, performing cross-over plays and eluding the opponents' marking.

Equipment: Supply of balls, 11 + 11 players.

Area required: Half of soccer field.

Coaching methods: Inductive ➤➤ guided discovery.

Description of the offensive situations:
* 10 throws in, pretending to pass the ball to his teammate 9 , who is sprinting towards him.
* 4 performs a cross-over play and rapidly moves forward to receive the ball from his teammate.
* he has at least two possibilities:
  1. controlling the ball and giving a cross towards the penalty spot for the upward penetration of 11 ;
  2. dribbling and crossing the ball towards the far angle of the goal area, where his teammate 3 is running.

Common mistakes: 4 makes the cross too late.

Coaching notes: _____

_____

_____

_____

_____

_____

Graphic

- - - - - - ▶	PATH OF THE PLAYER WITHOUT THE BALL
───────▶	PATH OF THE BALL
∿∿∿∿▶	DRIBBLE
1, **2**, **3**,..........	ATTACKING PLAYER
❶, ❷, ❸,..........	DEFENDING PLAYER
□ ○ ───────▶	ATTACKING PLAYER WITH THE BALL
●]	FEINT
●[	SCREEN

Restarting the game at set plays:
Throw-in #4

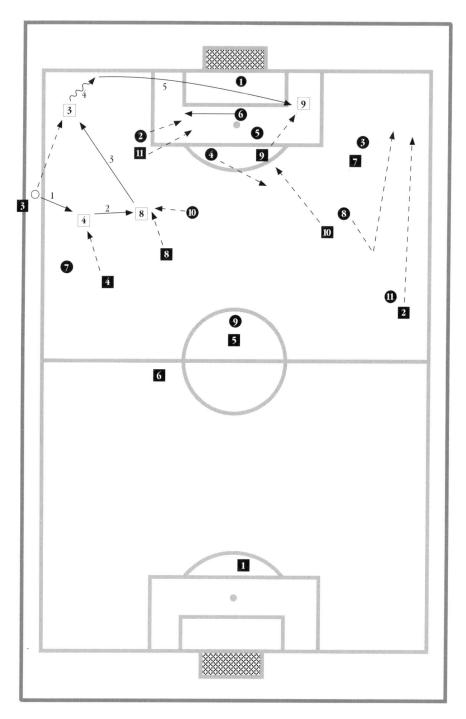

Technical-tactical purposes:
Throw-in from the offensive third of the field, eluding the opponents' marking upward and sideways.

Equipment: Supply of balls, 11 + 11 players.

Area required: Half of soccer field.

Coaching methods: Deductive ➤➤ assigned tasks.

Description of the offensive situations:
- ⬛3 throws in directing the ball towards ⬛4 , who is running from behind;
- ⬛4 gives a quick pass to ⬛8 ,
- ⬛8 controls the ball and gives a diagonal pass for the upward penetration of ⬛3 .
- ⬛3 dribbles the ball as far as the goal line and makes a cross towards the right angle of the 6 yard box,
- where ⬛9 is running to shoot at goal.

Common mistakes: Inaccuracy of the final pass.

Coaching notes: _____

_____

_____

_____

_____

_____

_____

_____

Graphic

– – – – – ►	PATH OF THE PLAYER WITHOUT THE BALL
─────►	PATH OF THE BALL
∿∿∿►	DRIBBLE
1, **2**, **3**,..........	ATTACKING PLAYER
❶, ❷, ❸,..........	DEFENDING PLAYER
☐○─────►	ATTACKING PLAYER WITH THE BALL
●]	FEINT
●[	SCREEN

Restarting the game at set plays:
Throw-in #5

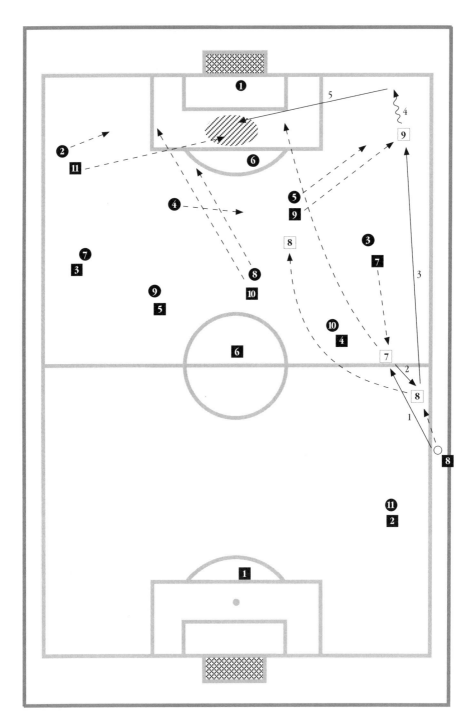

Technical-tactical purposes:
Throw-in in the first defensive third of the field, on the right side; inward overlapping runs.

Equipment: Supply of balls, 11 + 11 players.

Area required: Regulation soccer field.

Coaching methods: Deductive ➻ assigned tasks.

Description of the offensive situations:
* the player 8 throws the ball in.
* his teammate 7 rapidly sprints away from his opponent ③ ; he receives the ball and immediately plays it back to 8 .
* 8 makes a through pass for the cross-movement of his teammate 9 .
* 9 controls the ball and dribbles for some yards, then gives a cross towards the middle of the penalty area for 11 , who is sprinting from the left flank of the field.

Common mistakes: Throw-in is too hard or too high for the hard charging teammate to control.

Coaching notes: _____

_____
_____
_____
_____
_____
_____

Graphic
- - - - - - ▶ PATH OF THE PLAYER WITHOUT THE BALL
————▶ PATH OF THE BALL
∿∿∿▶ DRIBBLE
1, **2**, **3**,.......... ATTACKING PLAYER
❶, **❷**, **❸**,.......... DEFENDING PLAYER
▢ ○ ——▶ ATTACKING PLAYER WITH THE BALL
●] FEINT
●[SCREEN

Restarting the game at set plays:
Throw-in #6

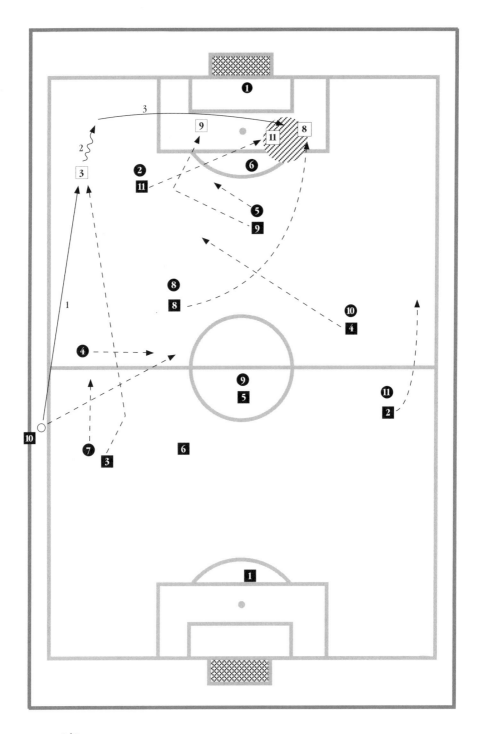

Technical-tactical purposes:
Throw-in from the first defensive third of the field, on the left side; inward overlapping runs.

Equipment: Supply of balls, 11 + 11 players.

Area required: Regulation soccer field.

Coaching methods: Deductive ➤ prescriptive.

Description of the offensive situations:
- 10 throws the ball in.
- 3 feints a diagonal run and then rapidly moves forward to receive the ball from his teammate; he controls it and dribbles for some yards,
- meanwhile, 8 moves upward, from the left to the right,
- while 9 runs in the opposite direction, performing a cross-over play with 11.
- 3 crosses the ball towards the penalty spot,
- where both 8 and 11 are ready to shoot at goal.

Common mistakes: Timing of runs either too early or too late.

Coaching notes: _____

_____

_____

_____

_____

_____

_____

Graphic

- - - - - ►	PATH OF THE PLAYER WITHOUT THE BALL
─────►	PATH OF THE BALL
∿∿∿►	DRIBBLE
1, **2**, **3**,..........	ATTACKING PLAYER
❶, ❷, ❸,..........	DEFENDING PLAYER
☐ o ────►	ATTACKING PLAYER WITH THE BALL
●]	FEINT
●[	SCREEN

Restarting the game at set plays:
Throw-in #7

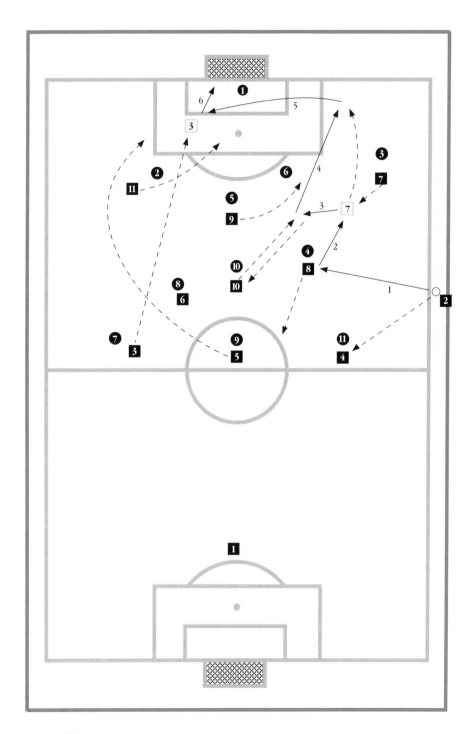

Technical-tactical purposes:
Throw-in from the second third of the field, on the right side; cross-over play and quick runs.

Equipment: Supply of balls, 11 + 11 players.

Area required: Half of soccer field.

Coaching methods: Deductive ➻ assigned tasks.

Description of the offensive situations:
- 2 throws the ball to 8, who directly plays it to the running 7;
- 7 passes the ball to his teammate 10, who is moving towards him;
- 10 controls the ball and gives a diagonal pass back to 7;
- 11 rapidly withdraws towards the midfield, while 3 and 5 sprint upward from a back position,
- 11 converges towards the penalty spot,
- 3 receives the ball from 7 and shoots at goal.
- 5, 11, 9 are ready to intervene to exploit a possible short clearance by the goalkeeper.

Common mistakes: Attacking runs by the defenders made too early or too late.

Coaching notes: ______________________________

____

____

____

____

____

Graphic

- - - - - - - - ► PATH OF THE PLAYER WITHOUT THE BALL
————————► PATH OF THE BALL
∿∿∿∿► DRIBBLE
1, 2, 3,......... ATTACKING PLAYER
❶, ❷, ❸,......... DEFENDING PLAYER
□ ○ ————► ATTACKING PLAYER WITH THE BALL
●] FEINT
●[SCREEN

Restarting the game at set plays:
Throw-in #8

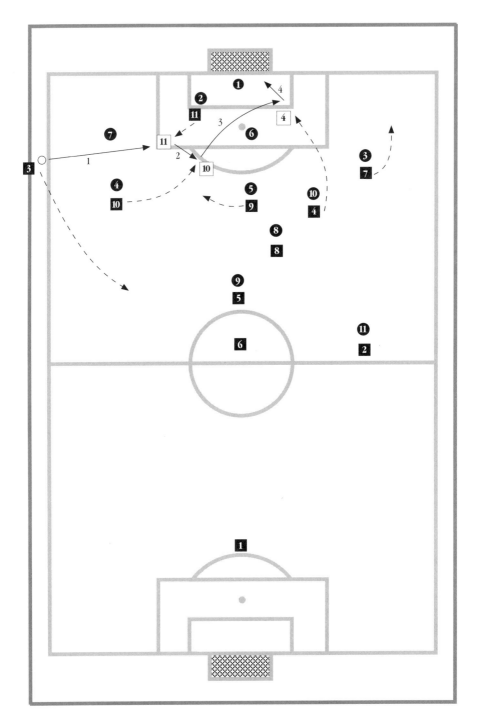

Technical-tactical purposes:
Throw-in from the offensive third of the field, in line with the edge of the opposing penalty area; shooting at goal after three passes.

Equipment: Supply of balls, 11 + 11 players.

Area required: Half of soccer field.

Coaching methods: Deductive ➡ prescriptive.

Description of the offensive situations:
- 3 throws the ball to his teammate 11, who is running towards him;
- 11 plays the ball to 10, who rapidly sprints to the edge of the penalty area and makes a diagonal pass for 4;
- 4 shoots at goal, heading the ball or kicking it.

Common mistakes: 10 makes his run too early, disrupting the timing of the play.

Coaching notes: _____

_____

_____

_____

_____

_____

_____

_____

Graphic

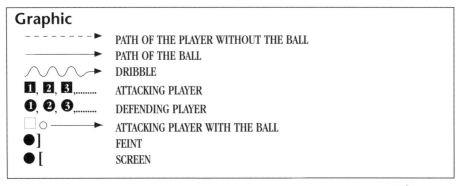

- - - - - - -►	PATH OF THE PLAYER WITHOUT THE BALL
————►	PATH OF THE BALL
∿∿∿►	DRIBBLE
1, **2**, **3**,........	ATTACKING PLAYER
❶, **❷**, **❸**,........	DEFENDING PLAYER
☐ ○ ————►	ATTACKING PLAYER WITH THE BALL
●]	FEINT
●[	SCREEN

Restarting the game at set plays:
Throw-in #9

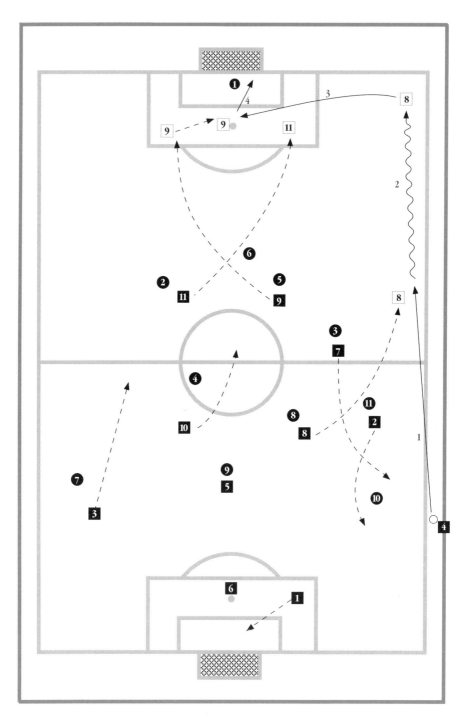

Technical-tactical purposes:
Throw-in from the first defensive third of the field, on the right side; eluding the opponents' marking, dribbling, crossing and shooting.

Equipment: Supply of balls, 11 + 11 players.

Area required: Regulation soccer field.

Coaching methods: Deductive ➤ assigned tasks.

Description of the offensive situations:
- 4 restarts the game with a throw-in.
- 2 and 7 run towards 4 ; in this way, they create space for the upward penetration of their teammate 8 on the right flank. He receives the ball and dribbles as far as the goal line;
- from this position, he gives a cross towards the penalty spot for 9 , who sprints in to the 18 yard box after performing a cross-over run with his teammate 11 , thus eluding their opponents' marking;
- 9 shoots at goal.

Common mistakes: Difficulty in controlling the long throw-in

Coaching notes: _____

_____
_____
_____
_____
_____
_____

Graphic

- - - - - ➤	PATH OF THE PLAYER WITHOUT THE BALL
⟶	PATH OF THE BALL
∿∿∿➤	DRIBBLE
1, **2**, **3**,........	ATTACKING PLAYER
❶, ❷, ❸,........	DEFENDING PLAYER
□ ○ ⟶	ATTACKING PLAYER WITH THE BALL
●]	FEINT
●[	SCREEN

Restarting the game at set plays:
Throw-in #10

Technical-tactical purposes:
Throw-in from the second defensive third of the field, on the left side; performing cross-over plays and eluding the opponents' marking at midfield.

Equipment: Supply of balls, 11 + 11 players.

Area required: Regulation soccer field.

Coaching methods: Deductive ➤➤ assigned tasks.

Description of the offensive situations:
- ☐3 restarts the game with a throw-in;
- ☐3 delivers the ball to ☐5 ;
- ☐5 plays the ball to ☐11 , who gives a quick pass to the running ☐7 .
- meanwhile, ☐3 sprints upward on the left flank of the field and receives a through pass from his teammate ☐7 .
- as soon as possible ☐3 gives a cross to ☐9 , who is waiting for the ball in the penalty area,
- ☐9 feints a short run and then rapidly moves towards the opposite horizontal goal line, ready to shoot at goal.

Common mistakes: Players have difficulty in losing their markers to break free into the penalty area.

Coaching notes: _____

_____

_____

_____

_____

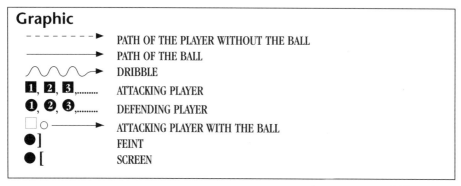

Graphic

- - - - - - ➤	PATH OF THE PLAYER WITHOUT THE BALL
──────➤	PATH OF THE BALL
∿∿∿➤	DRIBBLE
■1, ■2, ■3,..........	ATTACKING PLAYER
●1, ●2, ●3,..........	DEFENDING PLAYER
☐ ○ ──────➤	ATTACKING PLAYER WITH THE BALL
●]	FEINT
●[	SCREEN

Restarting the game at set plays:
Throw-in #11

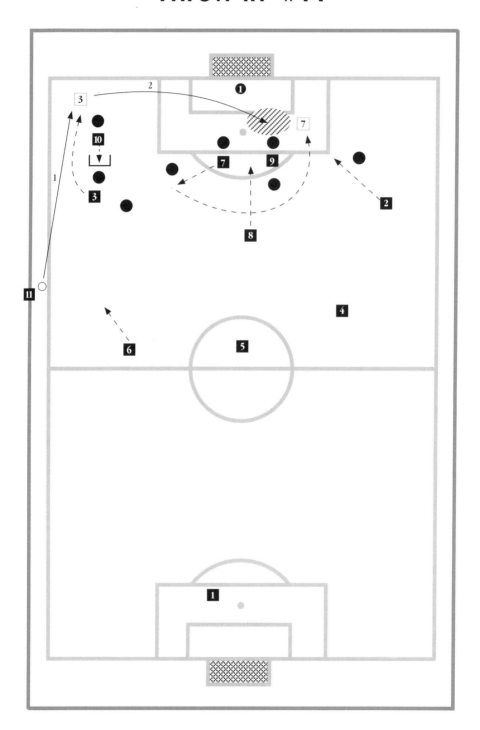

Technical-tactical purposes:
Throw-in from the offensive third of the field, with screen.

Equipment: Supply of balls, 11 + 11 players.

Area required: Half of soccer field.

Coaching methods: Deductive ➤ prescriptive.

Description of the offensive situations:
- 11 restarts the game with a throw-in.
- 10 moves towards the defender of his teammate 3 in order to perform the screen.
- in this way, 3 can make an outward overlapping run to receive the ball from 11 .
- in the meantime, the players 7 , 8 , 9 and 2 synchronize their moves outside the penalty area so as to cover tactical positions from which they could successfully shoot at goal.

Common mistakes: Tendency for attackers to overcrowd an area, causing confusion.

Coaching notes: _____

_____

_____

_____

_____

_____

_____

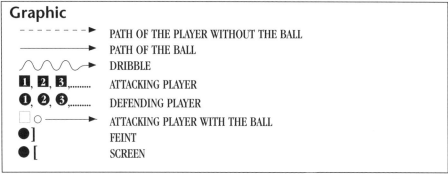

Graphic
- - - - - - - ►	PATH OF THE PLAYER WITHOUT THE BALL
─────────►	PATH OF THE BALL
∿∿∿►	DRIBBLE
1, **2**, **3**,.........	ATTACKING PLAYER
❶, ❷, ❸,.........	DEFENDING PLAYER
☐○ ─────►	ATTACKING PLAYER WITH THE BALL
●]	FEINT
●[	SCREEN

Restarting the game at set plays:
Throw-in #12

Technical-tactical purposes:
Throw-in on the left side of the field, in the defensive half; creating space for an upward movement on the left flank.

Equipment: Supply of balls, 11 + 11 players.

Area required: Regulation soccer field.

Coaching methods: Deductive ➺ assigned tasks.

Description of the offensive situations:
- 3 restarts the game with a throw-in. He fakes a pass to his teammate 6 , but then plays the ball to 10 , who is running backward to meet it,
- 10 directly plays the ball back to 3 .
- meanwhile, the player 6 makes an overlapping run on the left wing of the field and receives a pass by 3 .
- at the edge of the penalty area, the two strikers 9 and 11 cross each other and they are ready to receive the cross from the left
- the player who is standing in the best position can shoot at goal; the other one follows the action and runs to meet the ball in case the goalkeeper clears it.

Common mistakes: 3 fails to re-enter the playing field quickly enough.

Coaching notes: _____

_____

_____

_____

_____

Graphic
– – – – – –▶	PATH OF THE PLAYER WITHOUT THE BALL
──────▶	PATH OF THE BALL
∿∿∿∿▶	DRIBBLE
1, **2**, **3**,.........	ATTACKING PLAYER
❶, ❷, ❸,.........	DEFENDING PLAYER
☐ ○ ──────▶	ATTACKING PLAYER WITH THE BALL
●]	FEINT
●[	SCREEN

Restarting the game at set plays:
Throw-in #13

Technical-tactical purposes:
Throw-in from a position near the halfway line, on the left side of the field; clearing the space in the middle by means of feints.

Equipment: Supply of balls, 11 + 11 players.

Area required: Regulation soccer field.

Coaching methods: Deductive ➻ prescriptive.

Description of the offensive situations:
- 3 restarts the game with a throw-in.
- 10 performs a feint movement helping his teammate 11 to elude his opponent's marking; in this way, 11 can freely run in a central position to receive the ball from 3.
- 11 has different solutions to adopt:
  a. giving a through pass to 9;
  b. running alone towards the penalty area, dribbling the ball;
  c. playing the ball towards the right angle of the penalty area for his teammate 2, who is running from behind.

Common mistakes: 11 holds the ball too long, disrupting the timing of his teammates' runs.

Coaching notes: _____

_____

_____

_____

_____

_____

Graphic

– – – – – – ►	PATH OF THE PLAYER WITHOUT THE BALL
──────►	PATH OF THE BALL
∿∿∿►	DRIBBLE
1, **2**, **3**,.........	ATTACKING PLAYER
❶, ❷, ❸,.........	DEFENDING PLAYER
▢○────►	ATTACKING PLAYER WITH THE BALL
●]	FEINT
●[	SCREEN

DEFENSIVE WALLS

We have observed that restarting the game at set plays is particularly important from a tactical point of view during every team's performance. Therefore, covering the defensive area in the proper way is also fundamental.

For this reason, as soon as a team is awarded a free kick, the defensive side should pay particular attention not to be caught unawares.

All the players, or nearly all of them, should retreat in order to restore a proper defensive balance; if they gain possession of the ball, they must concentrate in order to be ready to begin a dangerous and unexpected counter-attack immediately.

It is very important to set the defensive wall accurately, as if it were an unsurmountable bulwark (defensive wall #1).

The arrangements "2+2", "3+2", "4+1" allow the defending team to cover both the areas in front of the two posts, so that the goalkeeper can stand in a central position.

In case of a corner kick against, it is possible to use a 'zone' defense, whose main advantage lies in the possibility to create an effective defensive triangle just where the ball is played.

Lineup and number of players in the defensive wall

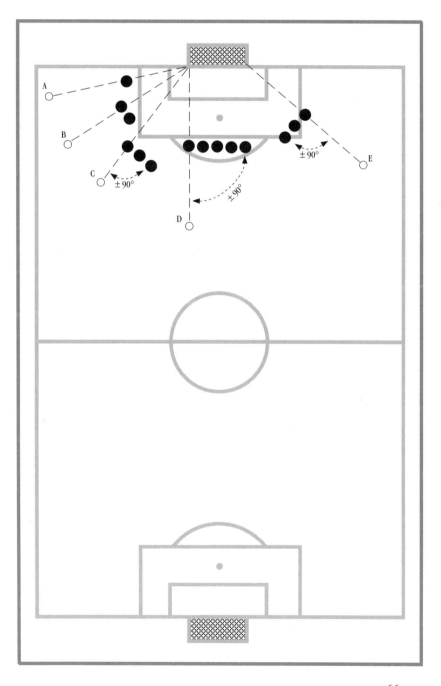

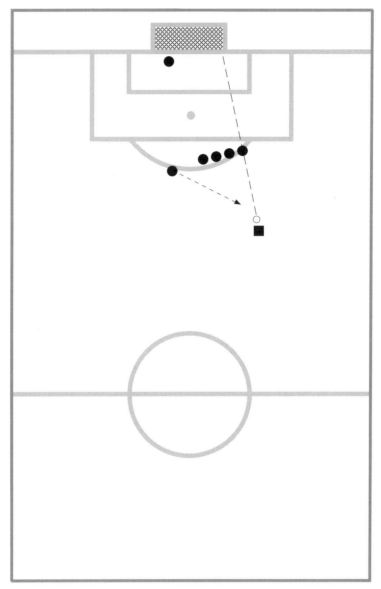

WALL 4+1 AT A DIRECT FREE KICK

The four players standing in the defensive wall are very close; the two play-ers in the middle are the tallest ones if the forward kicks the ball with the left foot. If he kicks with the right foot, the tallest player stands on the line post/ball. In case the opponent is particularly skilful at shooting the ball over the wall, the four defenders should be ready to jump, all together at the same time, or to stand on tiptoe. It is very important to choose the right moment to jump in order not to allow the opponents to shoot at goal with a ground shot under the wall. The player standing alone by the wall runs towards the ball. He should be less apprehensive, more rapid and more courageous than his teammates.

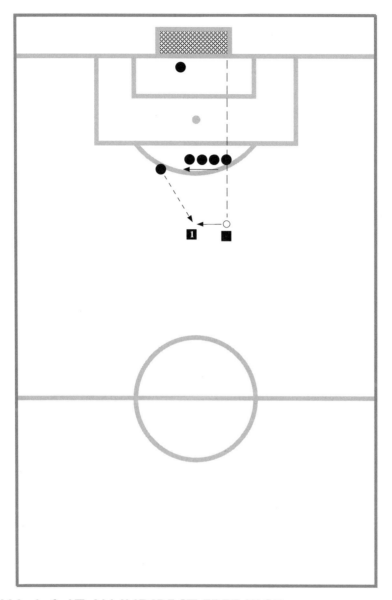

WALL 4+1 AT AN INDIRECT FREE KICK

The four players standing in the defensive wall are ready to take a side-step to the right, all together at the same time, in case the ball is played sideways to the player standing to the left of the place kicker. The player standing alone by the wall should immediately and fearlessly sprint towards the moving ball.

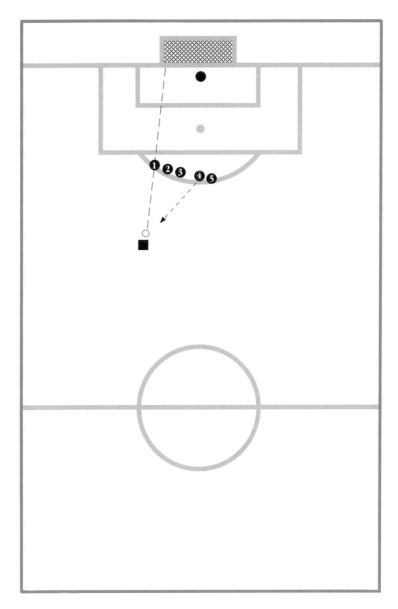

WALL 3+2 AT A DIRECT FREE KICK

The arrangement of the defensive wall should help the defending team to cover both the posts, thus leaving free space for the goalkeeper in the central position. The players should behave in the same way as in the wall 4+1.

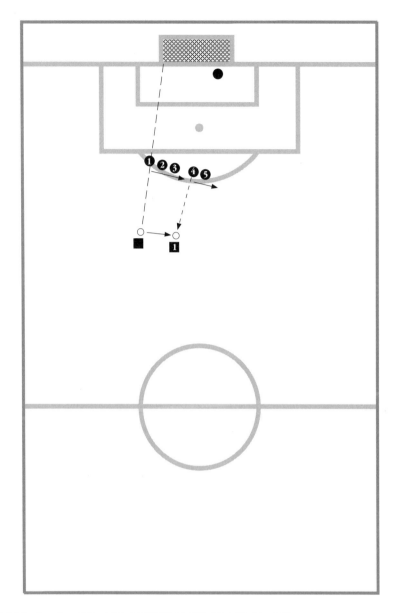

WALL 3+2 AT AN INDIRECT FREE KICK

In case of an indirect shot with the first pass given towards the inside of the field, the three players standing in the wall take a side-step, all together at the same time, while the fourth teammate sprints towards the ball (sliding tackle) in order to prevent a possible ground shot. The fifth player runs towards the ball, always trying to cover the area of the post. In case the opponents make a sideways pass, the three and the two players standing in the defensive wall take a side-step to the left simultaneously.

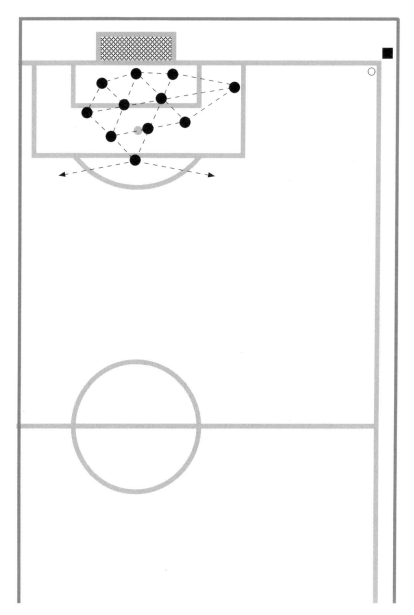

'ZONE' ARRANGEMENT AT A CORNER KICK

All the players of the defending team position themselves within the penalty area, trying to cover all the dangerous spaces. After the corner kick is taken, every player should look for the ball in his own space, trying to meet it with the greatest concentration and determination. As soon as the ball is kicked, the opponents in possession should be pressed immediately.

CONCLUSION

In this book we have expressly shown you mixed-type exercises, i.e.: some of them are based on technical-tactical solutions requiring the participation of all the players on the field (11+11), while other exercises are shown in an 'open' way, with a smaller number of players involved and multiple solutions suggested.

Our intent is to stimulate the coach-reader to use his own imagination, as well as the creativity of his players, to work out the best solutions in every specific situation.

Since soccer is an acyclic sport requiring particular skills to be applied in a number of different situations, it is advisable for a team to train for many different situations to restart the game at set plays. In this way, the strategy of the team cannot be foreseen by the opponents and, last but not least, a coach can always stimulate the attention and the concentration of his own players, who should be opportunely trained to take the decisive initiative during the set-up (who kicks the ball, how to kick, the right moment to shoot, the direction, the path of the ball, etc.).

The coach usually conveys a non-verbal message, conventionally known by all the players, to the captain of the team or to the player nearest the ball. However, he should not impose his own choice, but only help to suggest a possible tactical solution that his players will undoubtedly take into consideration for their final decision.

Some coaches prefer to entrust the setting of the defensive wall to their goalkeeper; others, and we belong to this group, think it better to give this responsibility to the player on the first post (the tallest one). For this reason, the goalkeeper should not leave the area near the far post unguarded.

It is possible to learn specific tactical movements for the restarting of the game at set plays according to different manners and purposes, synthesized as follows:
- in order to improve specific tactical skills, the training session should be based on analytical exercises involving only some players

- in order to assimilate tactical schemes concerning the whole of the team, it is useful to freeze the game repeatedly and in different positions of the field during the training session or in friendly games.

OBSERVING ➤ UNDERSTANDING ➤ CHOOSING ➤ PERFORMING

We do hope that this book can offer you a wide range of incentives and solutions concerning the restarting of the game at set plays.

We suggest to every coach not to give up the useful and satisfying habit of didactic planning; this method should aim at improving and consolidating those general and specific goals concerning technical-tactical skills. Moreover, we recommend to focus the attention on real play situations during the training session so as to help players to get accustomed to the reality of a competition.

Ad maiora!

GLOSSARY

Anticipation: ability to find tactical solutions before one's opponent; this is a very important characteristic in modern soccer and it requires promptitude, rapidity and accuracy at the same time.

Applied technical skill: referring to one or more technical gestures, aimed at one single tactical goal.

Balance: ability to maintain the right position in space, at every moment and in every movement; it also refers to the ability to restore these conditions in the shortest time as possible, in case external forces modify its starting condition.

Basic technical skill: the ability to perform single technical gestures; it concerns only the player playing the ball.

Charge: voluntary screen, performed with the body, to the movement of one's opponent.

Conditioned game: the fourth phase of the training session; it is a practice session or game, also a small-sided game, containing specific rules in relation to the goal to be achieved.

Corner kick: one of the ways to restart the game from a specific area of the field: the corner area.

Counterattack: referring to the action of a defending team which suddenly wins possession of the ball, reverses the play situation and rapidly creates an offensive combination.

Defensive diagonal: defensive tactical scheme performed when the opponent in possession of the ball moves on either of the two wings of the field.

Defensive wall: line-up of one, two or more players, aimed at reducing the area of the goal available for a successful shot at goal, particularly at free kicks.

Double screen: screen simultaneously performed by two players for the same teammate.

Feint: movement aimed at interrupting the defensive play of an opponent.

Free kick: direct or indirect kick awarded by the referee to one team whenever an opponent fouls outside the penalty area.

Give-and-follow: play the ball and follow its movement to perform a feint or an screen, or to exploit the feint of the teammate in possession.

Give-and-go: play the ball and move upward to receive a back-pass.

Goal area: marked rectangular area in front of each goal, with a depth of 6 yards.

Goal kick: kick by the defending team to restart the game after the attacking team has sent the ball over the goal line.

Individual tactical skill: referring to two or more technical skills aimed at a particular tactical purpose.

Individual technical skill: all the movements, with or without the ball, performed during a match, in accordance with the laws of the game.

Kick-off: place kick taken towards the opposite half of the field at the beginning of a match, at the beginning of the second half or when re-starting the game after a goal has been scored.

L-defense: referring to two defenders, one positioned in front of the player in possession in order to prevent him from shooting or passing the ball; the other positioned behind him so as to hinder his forward movement.

Man-to-man defense: defensive tactical system where the opponents are systematically marked and controlled during the offensive phase.

Mixed-type defense: defensive tactical system combining both the man-to-man system and the zone defense with a certain flexibility.

Motor anticipation skill: ability which allows a player to overcome his difficulties in information processing, the refractory period following every decision and which involves one's abilities to foresee what will happen.

Motor capacity: individual disposition for a particular motor skill.

Motor combination: ability to perform different movements in sequence or simultaneously, including them in a harmoniously organized motor planning.

Motor skill: motor gesture which can be improved through constant repetitions, thus becoming completely automatic; it does not require the constant intervention of one's will.

Screen: movement aimed at preventing the defensive play of one's opponent.

Overlapping offensive strategy: tactical movement aimed at gaining space forward with the participation of all the attacking players.

Overlapping pass: intentional movement of the ball through 'give-and-go' and 'give-and-follow' (inward or outward).

Pass towards the 'blind area': ball played behind the last two defenders, so as to facilitate the movement of one's teammate towards the opposite goal to shoot.

Penalty area: marked rectangular area in front of each goal, within which a foul or an intentional offense by the defender is punished by awarding a penalty kick to the attacking team; it has a depth of 18 yards.

Penalty kick: free shot at goal awarded by the referee to the attacking team for a foul committed within the penalty area.

Play system: team strategy concerning the lineup of the players on the playing field (for instance: 4-4-2; 4-3-3; 3-5-2; 3-6-1; 3-3-3-1; ...)

Pressing: tactical anticipation action aimed at gaining possession of the ball and moving forward. It can be performed in the defensive third of the field, at midfield and in the offensive third: it is necessary to anticipate the players without the ball and to attack the player in possession.

Pressure: defensive tactical action; it is something between the remote marking of the player in possession of the ball and the real pressing (tactical screen).

Reaction: it can be simple, referring to the ability to respond to one single stimulus, and complex, which means the ability to respond to different simultaneous incentives with a suitable tactical action.

Sensorial-perceptive capacity: important pre-requisite of the individual performance, characterized by the more or less effective use of sensorial factors (sight, hearing, touch, vestibular and proprioceptive systems).

Shadow-play: tactical practice allowing players to create and imagine movements without real opposition, or with passive opposition.

Side preference: the side of one's body or the limb a player preferably uses.

Sliding: defensive tactical scheme which starts by observing the position of the attacking player in possession of the ball on the central line.

Soccer intelligence: ability to manage new situations and to solve problems not only thanks to one's experience, but also by understanding all the connections existing between the different technical-tactical elements of a particular play situation.

Soccer skill: application of specific and adaptable motor skills, according to the real situations of a competition and to the prospects of success previously experienced.

Synergy: combined action or activity of different players in the team; joint work aimed at achieving a common positive goal.

Tackle: skill to dispossess the player in possession of the ball.

Tactical thought: ability of the player to perceive, choose, decide and perform the most suitable movements, according to that particular tactical play situation.

Team strategy: all the strategies every team previously studies and trains in order to obtain a positive and successful performance.

Throw-in: one of the ways to re-start the game; the ball is delivered with the hands from one of the sidelines.

Transfer: ability to practice some exercises aimed at improving one particular skill, but which actually improve another one at the same time (for instance: playing ball with one foot improves also the ability of the other foot; observing somebody else play ball improves one's own ball playing...).

Transition: the act of immediately shifting from the defensive position to the offensive one and vice versa.

Trip: foul, act of catching one's foot on the foot of the player with the ball, causing him to stumble or fall, thus losing possession of the ball.

Two-footed player: player skilful at playing the ball with both his right and his left foot.

Warming-up: period of light, mainly aerobic exercises performed before the main part of the training session or before a match. It involves a series of specific goals: mental relaxation, an increase in the body temperature, an increase in the heartbeat and in the respiratory rhythm, complete control over one's motor skills previously acquired as well as the harmony within the team group.

Zone defense: defensive tactical system where every defender is asked to control a specific area of the field in relation to the position of the ball.

Other Books from REEDSWAIN

#785:
Complete Books of
Soccer Restart Plays
by Mario Bonfanti and
Angelo Pereni
$14.95

#154:
Coaching Soccer
by Bert van Lingen
$14.95

#177:
PRINCIPLES OF
Brazilian Soccer
by José Thadeu Goncalves
in cooperation with Prof. Julio Mazzei
$16.95

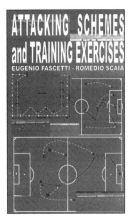

#185:
Conditioning
for Soccer
Dr. Raymond Verheijen
$19.95

#244:
Coaching the 4-4-2
by Maziali and Mora
$14.95

#765:
Attacking Schemes
and Training
Exercises
by Eugenio Fascetti and
Romedio Scaia
$14.95

Call REEDSWAIN 1-800-331-5191

Other Books from REEDSWAIN

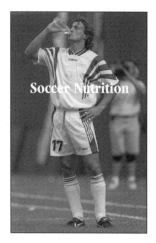

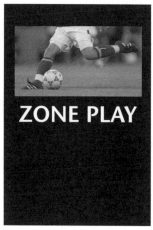

#786:
Soccer Nutrition
by Enrico Arcelli
$10.95

#788:
ZONE PLAY:
A Tactical and Technical
Handbook
$14.95

#267:
Developing
Soccer Players
THE DUTCH WAY
$12.95

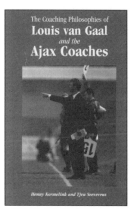

#175:
The Coaching Philosophies of
Louis van Gaal
and the
Ajax Coaches
by Kormelink and
Seeverens
$14.95

#284:
The Dutch
Coaching
Notebook
$14.95

#287:
Team Building
by Kormelink and
Seeverens
$9.95

Web Site: www.reedswain.com

NOTES

REEDSWAIN INC

BOOKS and VIDEOS

612 Pughtown Road

Spring City, Pennsylvania 19475 USA

1-800-331-5191 • www.reedswain.com

NOTES

REEDSWAIN INC
BOOKS and VIDEOS
612 Pughtown Road
Spring City, Pennsylvania 19475 USA
1-800-331-5191 • www.reedswain.com

NOTES

REEDSWAIN INC
BOOKS and VIDEOS
612 Pughtown Road
Spring City, Pennsylvania 19475 USA
1-800-331-5191 • www.reedswain.com